1989

University of St. Francis
GEN   181.06 S912
Strauss, Leo.
Philosophy and law :

W9-ADV-272

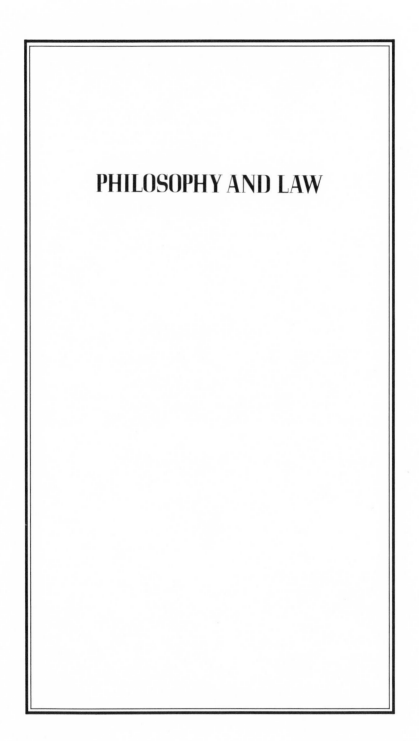

PHILOSOPHY AND LAW

Translated from the German by

Fred Baumann

Foreword by Ralph Lerner

THE JEWISH PUBLICATION SOCIETY

Philadelphia · New York · Jerusalem
5747 · 1987

LEO STRAUSS

PHILOSOPHY AND LAW

Essays Toward the Understanding of Maimonides and His Predecessors

LIBRARY
College of St. Francis
JOLIET, ILL.

Originally published in German under the title
Philosophie und Gesetz
Copyright © 1935 by Schocken Verlag, Berlin
Translation copyright © 1987 by The Jewish Publication Society
First English edition   All rights reserved
Manufactured in the United States of America
Library of Congress Cataloging in Publication Data
Strauss, Leo.
  Philosophy and Law.
  Translation of: Philosophie und Gesetz.
  Includes index.
  1. Philosophy, Jewish.   2. Law (Theology)
3. Maimonides, Moses, 1135–1204. Dalālat al-ḥā'irīn.
I. Title.
B757.L38S7613   1987   181'.06   86–19990
ISBN 0-8276-0273-1

Designed by Adrianne Onderdonk Dudden

181.06
5912

2-16-89 - Baker & Taylor - 877.21

134,978

To the Memory of Meyer Strauss

CONTENTS

FOREWORD

The usual offices of a foreword can safely be foregone in the present case. The author's own Introduction issues so powerful a challenge to contemporary enlightened opinion that it hardly needs another's seconding voice. An account of the context in which Leo Strauss came to write *Philosophy and Law* would be equally redundant. Of the desperate time when it first appeared in print, nothing need be said. Bare bibliographic facts suffice—Berlin: Schocken Verlag, 1935. And of its author as a young scholar and a Jew, nothing can be said beyond what he already has supplied himself. In the guise of introducing an English translation of his earliest published book, he composed an intellectual autobiography that lays bare the "theologico-political predicament" in whose grip he found himself and that had prompted these researches.[1] The authority of that account leaves little to be expected from the distant embellishments of others.

What might, however, bear brief comment here is the standing of *Philosophy and Law* in the larger body of Leo Strauss's work. At first glance, there appears to be adequate ground for slighting this book as an early effort, one soon to be superseded by deeper researches and maturer understanding. When, in the early 1960s, Strauss proceeded to restate some of the conclusions to which those researches had led him, he reported them as the result of "about twenty-five years of frequently interrupted but never abandoned study" of the *Guide of the Perplexed.*[2] In short, his settled conclusions about the *Guide* in particular, and Maimonides in general, depended on what he had come to learn since completing *Philosophy and Law.* He might well have said of this, his earlier reading of Maimonides, what he was to say of his earlier reading of Spinoza: ". . . I now read the *Theologico-political Treatise* differently than I read it when I was young. I understood Spinoza too literally because I did not read him literally enough."[3]

Yet such a judgment of the present work, plausible and even correct as far as it goes, fails to do justice to the way in which Strauss's life-long concerns shape the argument and tone of *Philosophy and Law.* One sees here—and often with a rhetorical power that Strauss rarely permitted himself to display in public—his passionate preoccupation with reopening questions that the certitudes of the age had pronounced settled or irrelevant. The powerful counterclaims of a revelation calling for obedience and a reason demanding satisfaction retained their primeval urgency for him. If others, seeking comfort or fleeing embarrassment, were led to muffle those counterclaims, that was not the case with Strauss. He sought, rather, to respect the gravity of those claims by retrieving them from their trivializers. But he also knew that reviving an argument long since embalmed, tagged, and shelved (whether by generally accepted opinion or by academic consensus) was in a way comparable to resurrecting the dead. Strauss never underestimated the difficulty of that task.

Less out of an accommodation to our age's openness to what it calls the lessons of History than by reason of a conviction that historical studies were indeed the necessary means of stirring those questions anew, Strauss proceeded early on to undertake a long series of such studies.[4] The present "Essays Toward Understanding" are of precisely that character. Yet the invigorating spirit of these pages is far removed from anything smacking of antiquarianism, on the one hand, or tendentious argumentation, on the other. For although the movement of the argument in *Philosophy and Law* looks like an archeologist's cautious unearthing and dusting-off of discrete strata and shards, the end in view is nothing less than a reconstructed edifice in its nobility and entirety. To see that whole, the spectator must first open his eyes, which in this context means being open to question, open to surprise. Yet that is precisely the state of mind that could not and, indeed, cannot be presumed.

The young Strauss saw with total clarity and unblinking steadiness the many ways in which a mind or an age might shield itself from questions and answers auguring to trouble its slumber. The guises available to prejudice in modern times—not the least of which bear the labels rationalism, science, and the like—make that always difficult act of self-liberation ever more trying, remote, and unlikely. To test by some other, earlier mode one's way of looking and asking requires first recovering that earlier way of looking on *its* terms. But here one falters at the very threshold of the undertaking. For the power of our prejudices, our neatly packaged (and hence concealed) presuppositions, comes between us and whatever it is we would understand from within. It is in this sense that Strauss could speak in *Philosophy and Law* of the need—peculiar to our modern situation—to ascend "out of the second, 'unnatural' cave (into which we have fallen . . .) into the first, 'natural' cave that Plato's image depicts, and the ascent from which, to the light, is the original meaning of philosophizing."[5]

These "essays toward the understanding of Maimonides and his predecessors" may, then, rightly be viewed as efforts to destroy a prevailing prejudice—namely, that modern rationalism had exploded or refuted the claims of orthodoxy, that science had overcome belief. Only when the reader recognizes this confident assertion for the prejudice it is, only with his ascent from out of the lower pit, is he at last free to begin his proper work in earnest. Only then is he in a position to recover those questions, in their classic simplicity and directness, which later sophistication may bury but never lay to rest.

Long passed was that "interval of calm, when the fight against Orthodoxy seemed to have been fought out and . . . the revolt of the forces unchained by the Enlightenment had still not broken out against their liberator; when, living in a habitable house, one could no longer see the foundation on which that house had been erected."[6] Strauss's readers of 1935 hardly stood in need of a reminder. For Jews in particular, the house had become a ruin and the dream of being at home a nightmare. Faced with the choice of an Orthodoxy affirming the God of Abraham, Creator of heaven and earth, or an unconditionally political (and therefore atheist) Zionism,[7] the modern Jew is left at an intolerable impasse. It is at this juncture that Strauss raised his heretical, even bizarre, suggestion. Every self-respecting Jew, confronted with the quandary just described and unable to accept wholeheartedly either the simple ancestral faith or its faithless antagonist, could only yearn for an enlightened Judaism to which he might cleave with heart and mind. It is a measure of Strauss's self-liberation and calm daring that he could bring this question into the open: Must enlightenment perforce be modern enlightenment?

Here Strauss turned to Maimonides, not in a spirit of pious solicitude, not as a caretaker of cherished antiquities, but as a serious-minded inquirer who is fully alive, fully awake, fully attentive. By making himself open to that great teacher's rationalism, Strauss also has made it easier for others (Jews and non-Jews) to find a standard by which to measure the pretensions of the age. With evident relish, he would refer to the lines with which Maimonides concluded his introduction to the first part of the *Guide:* "This, then, will be a key permitting one to enter places the gates to which were locked. And when these gates are opened and these places are entered into, the souls will find rest therein, the eyes will be delighted, and the bodies will be eased of their toil and of their labor."

Ralph Lerner

Notes

1. "Preface to the English Translation," *Spinoza's Critique of Religion* (New York: Schocken Books, 1965), pp. 1–31. This essay is reprinted in Leo Strauss, *Liberalism Ancient and Modern* (New York: Basic Books, Inc., 1968), pp. 224–257.

2. "How to Begin to Study *The Guide of the Perplexed*," an introductory essay to Moses Maimonides, *The Guide of the Perplexed*, translated by Shlomo Pines (Chicago: University of Chicago Press, 1963), p. xi. This essay is reprinted in *Liberalism Ancient and Modern*, pp. 140–184.

3. "Preface," *Spinoza's Critique of Religion*, p. 31.

4. In addition to the titles mentioned in the other notes to this Foreword, see *Natural Right and History* (Chicago: University of Chicago Press, 1953), and *What is Political Philosophy? and Other Studies* (Glencoe, Ill.: The Free Press, 1959).

5. Introduction, p. 112, n. 2. This theme is elaborated with great power in Strauss's analysis of "the petrified and self-complacent form of the self-criticism of the modern mind." See "How to Study Spinoza's *Theologico-Political Treatise*" (1948), reprinted in *Persecution and the Art of Writing* (Glencoe, Ill.: The Free Press, 1952), pp. 155–158.

6. Introduction, p. 16.

7. "A highly honorable but in the long and serious run an unsatisfactory answer" to what Enlightenment thinkers called "the Jewish question." Introduction, p. 19.

TRANSLATOR'S PREFACE

Among the notable contributions the late Professor Leo Strauss made to the study of the classics of political thought was his insistence on the authority of the text. It followed from this principle that one had initially to strive to understand a thinker as he understood himself and that as little as possible should obstruct one in that task. Ideally, one should read the work in the original, where striking problems that careful readers might discover at the surface, which would lead them to deeper levels of understanding, would not be concealed by translation. Thus, any effort to translate such a thinker's work should put literal accuracy above stylistic grace or, worse by far, helpful interpretation, so that the writer would speak, as much as possible, for himself and not through the mind of a translator.

When Professor Strauss's literary executor, Professor Joseph Cropsey, asked me to undertake the translation of *Philosophie und Gesetz*, it was perfectly clear to both of us that I would try my best to meet Professor Strauss's own standards in translating his book. Although some gracelessness of language has resulted, I am well aware that gracelessness in itself does not guarantee accuracy and that the translation may still have fallen short in many places. I know that I would have fallen even further short of the mark had it not been for the constant guidance and encouragement of Professor Cropsey, Professor Ralph Lerner and Professor Werner Dannhauser. I am particularly indebted to Professor Dannhauser for his careful eye and for his advice regarding specific formulations that had been used by Professor Strauss himself. Professor Lerner too has devoted a great deal of time and effort to aiding me in this project. I wish to thank the Institute for Educational Affairs for supporting the work of the translation. I am also greatly in the debt of Dr. Hillel Fradkin, who advised me on Hebrew and Arabic transliteration, on new editions of some of the critical works referred to by Professor Strauss, and on several points of substance. Without his help, I could not have completed this project. I am also grateful to M. Rémi Brague, who, working on a French translation, helped a great deal by alerting me to specific difficulties in the text. Any errors in the translation, of course, I must claim for my own.

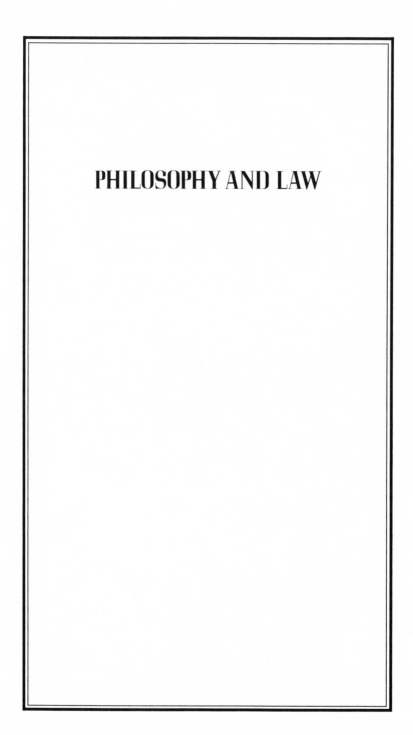

PHILOSOPHY AND LAW

INTRODUCTION

According to Hermann Cohen, Maimonides is the "classic of rationalism" in Judaism. This seems to us to be correct in a more exact sense than Cohen probably meant it. Maimonides' rationalism is the truly natural model, the standard that must be carefully guarded against every counterfeit, and the touchstone that puts modern rationalism to shame. The purpose of the present work is to arouse a prejudice in favor of this conception of Maimonides, or rather, to excite a suspicion against the powerful prejudice to the contrary.

Even someone who is free of all natural attraction to the past and who believes that the present has nothing to learn from the past because it is the age in which man has reached the highest stage of self-consciousness, yet, even such a one hits upon Maimonides' teaching as soon as he seriously tries to gain clarity about the present he thus appraises. For this attempt can only succeed if at every moment one confronts modern rationalism, understood as the source of the present, with medieval rationalism. If one undertakes such a confrontation seriously, freely asking which of the two opposed rationalisms is the true rationalism, then in carrying out that investigation, medieval rationalism (whose classic representative for us is Maimonides) becomes more than merely a means to achieve a sharper perception of the peculiarity of modern rationalism; it becomes the standard against which modern rationalism proves to be only apparent rationalism. In just this way the self-evident starting point—namely, that the self-knowledge of the present is a necessary and sensible enterprise—gains a non-self-evident justification. The critique of the present, the critique of modern rationalism,[1] understood as the critique of modern sophistry, is the necessary beginning, the constant accompaniment, and the unmistakable mark of that search for truth which is possible in our age.

The present condition of Judaism as such is determined by the Enlightenment, that is, abstracting from the basic constitution of Judaism that is not touched by and through the Enlightenment. For all the peculiar appearances of the present (if one does not let oneself be deceived by their foregrounds and pretexts) point back to the movement of the seventeenth and eighteenth centuries introduced by Descartes' *Meditations* and Hobbes' *Leviathan*, that is, back as though to their source, to the Enlightenment. This fact is hard to dispute; only its scope and meaning are disputable. For the presuppositions that the present and the age of the Enlightenment share have now become so self-evident that only, or especially, the contrast between the Enlightenment and the present is apt to be noticed and taken seriously. The Enlightenment seems to have been "overcome" long ago; its justified requests have become "trivial" and seem to have received their due; its "shallowness," on the other hand, seems to have fallen into deserved contempt.

Very far from our age lies the quarrel over the literal inspiration or the merely human character of Scripture, over the reality or impossibility of the biblical miracles, over the eternity and thus the immutability or the historical variability of the Law, over the creation or the eternity of the world. Now all arguments proceed on a plane on which the great issues of the quarrel between Enlightenment and Orthodoxy do not even have to be posed. In the end, these issues even have to be rejected as "wrongly posed." If that were all there was to it, then indeed the influence of the Enlightenment on Judaism would be as unworthy of serious consideration and care as all contemporary "movements" (though not all contemporaries, to be sure) assume. But are the presuppositions of the Enlightenment really trivial? Is the Enlightenment really a contemptible opponent?

If, on the other hand, the basis of the Jewish tradition is belief in the creation of the world, in the reality of biblical miracles, in the absolute obligation and the essential immutability of the Law as based on the revelation at Sinai, then one must say that the Enlightenment has undermined the foundation of the Jewish tradition. The radical Enlightenment (Spinoza comes to mind) did just this from the beginning, with full consciousness and full intent. And as far as the moderate Enlightenment is concerned, it soon had to expiate its efforts to mediate between Orthodoxy and the radical Enlightenment—between the belief in revelation and the belief in the self-sufficiency of reason—by suffering a contempt from which even the greatest fair-mindedness of historical judgment cannot save it.

The latecomers, who saw that the attacks of Hobbes, Spinoza, Bayle, Voltaire, and Reimarus could not be parried by defensive measures such as Moses Mendelssohn's, agreed, initially, with the radical Enlightenment as opposed to Orthodoxy. Thus, to start with, they conceded all the real or supposed results and all the explicit or implicit presuppositions of the critique of miracles and of the Bible. According to their own opinion, however, they restored the foundations of the tradition through the counterattack they launched against the (radical) Enlightenment. In other words, these later figures, who recognized that every compromise between Orthodoxy and Enlightenment is incapable of being sustained, moved from the plane on which Enlightenment and Orthodoxy had fought with each other (where the moderate Enlightenment had striven for a compromise) to another, "higher" plane, which as such made a synthesis of Enlightenment and Orthodoxy possible. On this newly gained plane, these later figures remade the foundations of the tradition, even though, as is inevitable with a synthesis, in a modified, "internalized" form.

It is not exactly difficult, however, to realize that the "internalization" of such concepts as Creation, Miracle, and Revelation robs them of their entire meaning. All that distinguishes the "internalizations" of these concepts from the denial of their significance are the intentions (if not good, in any case well-meaning) of their originators. If God did not create the world in an "external" sense, if He did not really create it, if Creation thus cannot be maintained even in its theoretical content as simply true, as the fact of Creation, then, for the sake of probity, one must deny the Creation or at least avoid talking about it. All "internalizations" of the basic assertions of the tradition have their basis in this: from the "reflected" presupposition, from the "higher" plane of the post-Enlightenment synthesis, the relation of God to nature cannot be understood any more and therefore cannot even be of interest any more.

These "internalizations," so much in use today, are in truth denials. This fact, manifest to the pristine open-minded view, is only obscured because we find ourselves initially, that is to say as long as we have not fought against our prejudices by historical reflection, wholly under the spell of the way of thought created by the Enlightenment and fortified by its successors or opponents. This bias shows itself especially in the way the "internalization" of the basic assertions of the Jewish tradition is justified. There seems to be no "internalization" of this kind for whose innocence one of the utterances of one of the traditional authorities cannot be found and brought forward as testimony. But even if one wholly ignores the unprincipled way in which expressions are torn from their context and frequently brought forward as decisive testimony, such assurances (which in truth are *ex post facto*) rest on one of two errors or on both at once. First, one calls up against the orthodox, "external" conception testimonies that belong to an undeveloped stage of the formulation of belief. In this way one can protect oneself, for example, against the teachings of literal inspiration, of the Creation as Creation *ex nihilo*, and of the immortality of the individual. Whenever these teachings first appeared in history, their relation to teachings of undisputed biblical origin is of such evident necessity that it is hard to cast doubt on them if one intends to remain in harmony with the "religion of the prophets." Insofar as one opposes the full expression of the Jewish tradition by calling on those of its elements that stand in the foreground of the Bible, and especially in the later prophets, one adheres to the method of the

Enlightenment, which has been recognized as authoritative above all by "religious liberalism." This fact is generally known, and since liberalism, partly for very good and partly for very bad reasons, recently has come into bad repute, the biblicistic, or rather the historical-critical, method of "overcoming" Orthodoxy is used ever more rarely.

Second, one calls up against Orthodoxy extreme expressions that have been ventured within the Jewish tradition. In this way, for example, one can protect oneself against the teachings of the absolute immutability of the Law and of miracles. But however well witnessed and repeated an extreme expression may be, a very "daring," very "free" expression, which (meant as daring) has as its firm ground the belief in Creation, Miracles, and Revelation that makes it possible in the first place, is one thing. According to its own meaning, such an expression is misunderstood, even perverted, if it is separated from this ground. Employing an expression founded in this way as a foundation itself is something else. Insofar as one makes an extreme expression (like a peak of a pyramid) into the foundation of the Jewish tradition, one proves again that one is wholly biased by the Enlightenment's way of thinking. For this is precisely the mark of the Enlightenment: Through a supposed or only allegedly "immanent" critique and development of the tradition, it makes the extremes of the tradition into the foundation of a position which, in truth, is wholly incompatible with the tradition.[2]

It must necessarily remain the case that the "internalization" of the fundamental assertions of the tradition robs them of their meaning, and that not just every compromise but also every synthesis between the opposed positions of Orthodoxy and Enlightenment proves to be untenable. Then it follows that the alternative of either Orthodoxy or Enlightenment can today no longer (or rather, not even yet) be avoided. If this is so, then one must at first and at least once descend to the level of the classical quarrel between Enlightenment and Orthodoxy where one fought and could fight over the one eternal truth, because the natural desire for truth had not yet been killed by the newer dogma that "religion" and "science" each aim at their own allotted "truth."

In order to reach this level, one does not have to remove oneself very far from the magic circle of the present. The radical Enlightenment is still alive today, and in a certain sense (namely, in reference to its ultimate and most extreme consequences), it is far more "radical" today than it was in the seventeenth and eighteenth centuries. Orthodoxy too is still alive today. The quarrel between Enlightenment and Orthodoxy, 'which is possible without further arrangements, must thus be repeated. Or rather, as one recognizes if one has not deliberately closed one's eyes, the long and still developing quarrel between Enlightenment and Orthodoxy must again be understood.

But has not the challenge for a repetition or a reunderstanding of this quarrel long since been silently met? Why, then, set into motion once more what has finally, finally, come to rest? Is not the critique of "internalizations," on which this challenge rests in the first instance, a case of forcing an open door? Was not the actual, although often hidden, impulse of the movement whose goal was the return to tradition and whose typical and unforgotten expression was the development, if not the teaching, of Hermann Cohen, precisely the insight into the questionable character of the "internalizations" with which the nineteenth century had in general soothed itself? Has not the condition of Judaism transformed itself wholly, through and through, during the last generation, thanks to that movement?

It must be granted that the condition of Judaism has been transformed as a consequence of the movement of return, but that it has been transformed through and through must be disputed. It was not transformed through and through[3] because in the whole course of the movement of return, fundamental reflection about the conflict between Enlightenment and Orthodoxy, fundamental revision of the results of that conflict, did not follow. And yet, according to the meaning of that movement, nothing would have been more necessary than such reflection and revision.

However, the most significant representatives of this orientation did not unreservedly undertake the return to tradition. Until the end, Cohen maintained explicit reservations about the tradition, in the name of freedom and of man's independence. And Franz Rosenzweig, who at least in a certain way went farther on Cohen's path than Cohen himself, left no doubt that he could adopt neither the traditional belief in immortality nor the allegedly characteristic concept of the Law held by German Orthodoxy. On closer inspection, we immediately recognize what neither Cohen nor Rosenzweig had scruples about admitting, namely, that these or related reservations[4] originate with the Enlightenment. But just because the return to tradition claims to stand in connection with a "new thinking," these reservations need a principled and connected justification upon that new basis. Yet no one will dare assert that these reservations received a justification (which would consequently be a partial justification of the Enlightenment) that would satisfy reasonable claims. Rather, the return to tradition was accomplished solely in arguments with the post-Enlightenment synthesis, especially with Hegel.[5]

It was thought that the direct and thematic argument with the Enlightenment might be avoided because (consistent with the sense of the Hegelianism one had "overcome") it was assumed that the Enlightenment had been "overcome" by "overcoming" the Hegelianism that had "transcended" it. In truth, however, the critique of Hegelianism was precisely what led accordingly to a rehabilitation of the Enlightenment. For what else but a rehabilitation of the Enlightenment was the critique on which the return to tradition rested; namely, the critique of the "internalizations" that the nineteenth century had carried out, following Lessing above all? If the assertions of the tradition have also and precisely an "external" meaning, then the Enlightenment's attack, which was after all directed only against the assertions of the tradition understood "externally," was not based on a principled misunderstanding of the tradition. Hobbes, Spinoza, and Voltaire would not and did not write a single line against the tradition's "inner" meaning.

This fact should have been conceded and emphasized. And since part of the Enlightenment critique of tradition was acceded to in a way that was unclear as to principles, it would also have had to be conceded and emphasized that the conflict between Enlightenment and Orthodoxy not only did not lack an object but also was in no way settled. All those who have attentively observed the movement under discussion, however, will attest that neither the one nor the other was conceded or emphasized.[6] Thus, exactly if the motive of this movement is justified, it wholly and especially depends on repeating or reunderstanding the classic quarrel between Enlightenment and Orthodoxy.

After all, this conflict has by no means been made groundless by the reputed "victory" of the Enlightenment over Orthodoxy. For one would have to be of the opinion that world history (actually just the history of two to three hundred years) is world judgment. In truth, however, as precisely the Enlightenment still knew, victories are "very ambiguous proofs of the just cause, or rather . . . are not at all," and therefore "he who wins the judgment and he who should win the judgment are only rarely the same person."[7]

If it depends on distinguishing between the party that won the judgment, that is, the Enlightenment, and the party that should have won the judgment, that is, by Lessing's rule, presumably Orthodoxy—in other words, if it depends on exercising the critique of the Enlightenment's victory over Orthodoxy, then, as things are, one has to bring out the dusty books that must be regarded as the classic documents of the quarrel between Enlightenment and Orthodoxy. And one must hear the arguments of both parties. Only if one does that or more precisely, only if one has the whole course of that quarrel before one's eyes, can one hope to be able to arrive at an unprejudiced view of both parties' concealed presuppositions and thereby at a reasonable judgment about the right and wrong of their quarrel.[8]

Critical testing of the arguments and counterarguments brought forth in this quarrel leads to the result that one cannot speak of a refutation of the fundamental assertions of the tradition understood "externally," because all these assertions rest on the irrefutable presupposition that God is omnipotent and that His will is unfathomable. If God is omnipotent, then miracles and revelation are possible as such, especially the miracles and revelation of the Bible. Orthodoxy, to be sure, and therefore also the Enlightenment, care less for the possibility or impossibility of the biblical miracles and Revelation than for their reality or unreality, but in fact, almost all the attempts of the Enlightenment to demonstrate the unreality of the biblical miracles and Revelation rest on the express or silent presupposition that the impossibility of miracles is simply established, or rather, is demonstrable.

Despite this, it was precisely the most radical Enlighteners who, in making their critique, experienced the fact that as a consequence of the irrefutability of the ultimate presupposition of Orthodoxy, all the individual assertions that rest on that presupposition are indestructible. If they did not recognize it clearly, in any case they felt it vividly. Nothing proves this more clearly than the weapon that did them such excellent service that it might even be said that it alone decided the victory of Enlightenment over Orthodoxy. This weapon is mockery. As Lessing, who must have known, said, by means of mockery they tried to "laugh" Orthodoxy out of a position from which no scriptural or rational proof could expel it.

The Enlightenment's mockery of the teachings of the tradition is thus not just the consequence of a previous refutation of these teachings. It does not express the astonishment of unprejudiced men at the power of plainly absurd prejudices; rather, mockery is the refutation. In mockery, the liberation from "prejudices" presumably already discarded is consummated for the very first time. At least, even if consequent, mockery is the decisive legitimation of a liberty won in whatever way.[9] Thus the significance of mockery for the Enlightenment's critique of religion is an indirect proof of the irrefutability of Orthodoxy. For that reason, Orthodoxy, unchanged in its essence, was able to outlast the attack of the Enlightenment and all later attacks and retreats.

Yet even though the attack of the Enlightenment upon Orthodoxy failed, the battle of the two hostile powers still had a highly consequential and positive result for the Enlightenment. It may provisionally be said that the Enlightenment succeeded for its part in defending itself against the attack of Orthodoxy. Let us take an example that is more than an example. Even if it could not prove the impossibility or the unreality of miracles, the Enlightenment could demonstrate the unknowability of miracles and thus protect itself against Orthodoxy's claims.

What holds for the aggressive critique of the Enlightenment thus does not hold for its defensive critique. The quarrel between Enlightenment and Orthodoxy made clearer and better known than before that the presuppositions of Orthodoxy (the reality of Creation, Miracles, and Revelation) are not known (philosophically or historically) but are only believed and thus lack the peculiarly obligatory character of the known. And not just this. Where pre-Enlightenment science was in a certain harmony with the teachings of faith, the new science, which had proved itself in the fight against Orthodoxy (even if it did not have its whole *raison d'être* in it) stood in an opposition to belief that was often concealed, always basically effective, and therefore always re-erupting.

The formation of the new science therefore led to the result that fundamental teachings of the tradition, which had also been counted as knowable under the presuppositions of the older science, came more and more to be viewed as merely believed. The destruction of natural theology and natural law, which, to say the least, was prepared in the age of Enlightenment, is the most important example and indeed the peculiar mark of this formation. Its final result is that unbelieving science and belief no longer have, as they did in the Middle Ages, a common basis in natural knowledge upon which a meaningful quarrel between belief and unbelief is possible. Rather, any understanding for even the possibility of an opposition between them was at the point of being lost. Orthodoxy really had no part in the world that was created by the Enlightenment and its heirs, the world of "modern culture." If it were to remain true to itself, it did not even have an entry into that world. It survived the nineteenth century, more despised than wondered at, as an uncomprehended remnant of a forgotten antiquity.

The Enlightenment thus did not allow the failure of its attack upon Orthodoxy to distract it in its reconstruction of the world. One must say rather that it was just because of this failure that the Enlightenment was compelled to reconstruct a world. For it did not wish to limit itself to discarding the assertions of Orthodoxy as not known but only believed. Under the impact of the claims of these assertions, the Enlightenment wanted to refute them. But the assertions that the world is the creation of an omnipotent God and therefore miracles are possible in it and that man needs revelation for the guidance of his life can be refuted neither by experience nor by the principle of contradiction. For experience does not speak against the guidance of this world and of man by an unfathomable God, and the concept of an unfathomable God does not contain a contradiction in itself. If one wished to refute Orthodoxy, no other way remained but to attempt a complete understanding of the world and life without the assumption of an unfathomable God. This means that the refutation of Orthodoxy depended on the success of a system. Man had to prove himself theoretically and practically the lord of the world and the lord of his life. The world he created had to make the world that was merely "given" to him disappear. Then Orthodoxy was more than refuted, it was "outlived." Inspired by the hope of "overcoming" Orthodoxy through completion of a system, the Enlightenment scarcely noticed the failure of its actual attack on Orthodoxy. Striving for victory by means of a truly Napoleonic strategy, the Enlightenment left in its rear the uncapturable fortress of Orthodoxy, saying to itself that the enemy would not and could not risk a sortie. Renouncing the impossible direct refutation of Orthodoxy, the Enlightenment turned to its own special project, civilizing the world and man. If this project had succeeded, there might perhaps not have been any need for further proof of the Enlightenment's right to victory over Orthodoxy, just as no further proof was believed to be necessary as long as it seemed to go well. But doubts about the successes of civilization soon became doubts about the possibility of civilization. Finally, the belief is dying out that man can always push back "natural limits" even farther, progress to ever greater "freedom," "subjugate" nature, "prescribe her laws," or "generate" her by the power of pure thought. In the end, what remains of the success of the Enlightenment? What finally does prove to be the basis and justification for this success?

Despite the opposite appearance, the Enlightenment's critique of Orthodoxy is in truth merely defensive. It is based on the radical renunciation of a refutation of Orthodoxy. The Enlightenment proved only the unknowability, not the impossibility, of miracles. To be more precise, it proved that miracles cannot be known on the basis of the new natural science. The actual grounds for the Enlightenment's right thus seem to be the new natural science.

In fact, it cannot be disputed that it was the belief that the science of Galileo, Descartes, and Newton had refuted the science of Aristotle and the "natural world image" that it had explicated and which is also the Bible's "world image" that was initially decisive for the success of the Enlightenment. The reconciliations between the "modern world image" and the Bible, which shot up like weeds in the seventeenth and eighteenth centuries and are attempted often enough even today, only delayed that success and did not call it into question. For these reconciliations always work ultimately as vehicles of the Enlightenment, not as dams against it. The moderate Enlightenment is the best first harvest of the radical Enlightenment. Made acceptable by the moderate Enlightenment, the new natural science entered upon its victorious campaign as the ally and pioneer of the radical Enlightenment.

But precisely this new science could not long uphold the claim to have brought to light the truth about the world "in itself"; its "idealistic" explication already informs its beginnings.[10] Modern "idealism" fulfills itself, on the one hand, in the discovery of the "aesthetic" as the purest insight into the creativity of man, and on the other hand in the discovery of the radical "historicity" of man and his world as the final overcoming of even the idea of an eternal nature, an eternal truth. Finally, it understands modern natural science as a historically conditioned form of "world interpretation" along with others; thereby it makes possible the rehabilitation of the "natural world view" on which the Bible is based.

Therefore, as soon as modern "idealism" has fully won out, the victory of Enlightenment over Orthodoxy loses its originally decisive justification. The proof that miracles cannot be known as such becomes powerless. For miracles as such are unknowable only on the presuppositions of modern natural science. As long as this science was deemed the only path to the one truth, one could rely on the view, attested to by historical research, that the assertion of miracles is relative to the prescientific state of mankind and thus has no dignity whatsoever. But it finally appears that the facts that attest to this view allow an opposite interpretation. In the end, is not the ground of just that concept of science that guides modern science the intention to protect oneself radically against miracles? Was not the "unique" "world interpretation" of modern natural science, according to which miracles are admittedly unknowable, thought through so that miracles would be unknowable, so that man would be protected from the grasp of the omnipotent God?

Thus modern natural science could be the foundation or the means of the victory of the Enlightenment over Orthodoxy only as long as the old concept of truth, which the Enlightenment had already destroyed, still ruled the dispositions of men, and especially as long as it determined the view one had of modern natural science. Only because of this was the attempt to ground the modern ideal, the ideal of civilization by means of modern natural science, temporarily possible. It was believed that the new concept of nature was the adequate foundation of the old ideal. But this was a delusion. One was forced to ascertain that the "goal- and value-free" nature of modern natural science could tell man nothing about "ends and values," that the "Is," understood in the sense of modern natural science, contains no reference whatsoever to the "Ought" and thus that the traditional view that the right life is a life according to nature becomes meaningless on the basis of modern presuppositions.[11]

If, therefore, modern natural science cannot justify the modern ideal, and if, correspondingly, the connection between the modern ideal and modern natural science is unmistakable, then the question must be posed whether, on the contrary, the modern ideal is in truth not the ground of modern natural science, and whether it is not also precisely a new belief rather than a new knowledge that justifies the Enlightenment.

If the question is posed in this form, it loses the taint that understandably clings to the question about the moral origins of modern natural science. For even the most believing adherents of this science admit that the rise of a new ideal (a new representation of the correct life of man) was decisive for the victory of Enlightenment over Orthodoxy, even if it only followed the success of natural science. Indeed, according to their view, the ideal of Freedom, understood as the autonomy of man and his culture, has this significance. But this view can be maintained only if one confuses "freedom," understood as autonomy, with the "freedom" of conscience, the "freedom" of philosophizing, political "freedom" or the ideal of autarky of the philosophical tradition.

Freedom, understood as the autonomy of man and his culture, is neither the original nor the eventual justification of the Enlightenment. Rather, this ideal was only viable during an interval of calm, when the fight against Orthodoxy seemed to have been fought out and, correspondingly, the revolt of the forces unchained by the Enlightenment had still not broken out against their liberator. This was the interval when, living in a habitable house, one could no longer see the foundation on which that house had been erected. In that epoch, after the final entrance into the state of civilization, one could forget the state of nature that alone could legitimize civilization and therefore one could set the "higher" ideal of culture, understood as the sovereign creation of spirit, in place of the elementary ideal of civilization, understood as the self-assertion of man against an over-powerful nature.

The Jewish tradition answers the question of the original ideal of the Enlightenment more adequately than the philosophy of culture. In many if not all cases, the Jewish tradition characterizes apostasy from the Law and rebellion against the Law as Epicureanism. Whatever facts, impressions, or suspicions may have led the rabbis to this characterization and attribution of apostasy, it is corroborated by historical investigation of the original Epicureanism. Epicurus truly epitomizes the classic critique of religion. Like no other, his whole philosophy presupposes that the danger threatening the happiness and repose of men is the fear of supernatural powers and death.

Indeed, this philosophy is scarcely anything else but the classical means to calm the fear of the *numen* and of death by showing them to be "without object."

The influence of the Epicurean critique on the Enlightenment shows itself if one follows the traces of the Enlightenment step by step from its beginnings up to Anatole France. The Epicurean critique is the foundation, or rather the foreground, of the Enlightenment critique. The Epicurean critique thus experiences an essential transformation in the age of the Enlightenment. The Enlightenment, to be sure, is also and especially concerned with the happiness and repose of man, which it sees threatened primarily or exclusively by religious imaginings. However, the Enlightenment understands this happy repose fundamentally differently from the original Epicureans; it understands "peace" in such a way that for it, the civilization, subjection, and improvement of nature—especially human nature—become necessary. While it was the fearfulness of the fearful delusion of religion that animated the struggles of the Epicureans against it, it was the delusionary character of that delusion that the Enlightenment especially aimed at. It does not matter whether religious imaginings are fearful or consoling; as delusions, they deceive men about the real goods and past the enjoyment of the real goods; they divert them away from the real "this-worldliness" to an imaginary "otherworldliness." Men are so misled that they allow a greedy clergy, which "lives" on these delusions, to cheat them of the possession and enjoyment of the real "this-worldly" goods.

Once freed from religious delusions, awakened to a sober recognition of his real situation, and instructed by bad experiences about the threat posed to him by a meager, hostile nature, man recognizes that his sole salvation and duty are not so much "to cultivate his garden" as rather first of all to procure a "garden" for himself by making himself the lord and possessor of nature.

Of course this "crude" conception has long since been "overcome" by one that fully reveals the tendency that announces and betrays itself in the turn from Epicureanism to Enlightenment. Its last and purest expression is that religious imaginings are rejected not because they are fearful but because they are desirable, because they are consoling. It is not as if religion were a tool, created by man for dark reasons in order to torment himself or to burden his life unnecessarily; rather, it is an escape man has taken for transparent reasons, in order to avoid that terror and hopelessness of life that no advance of civilization can destroy, in order to make life easier to bear.

The last and purest basis of justification for the revolt against the tradition of revelation in the end turns out to be a new form of bravery. It forbids every flight from the horror of life into consoling illusion. It rather takes the eloquent depictions of the misery of man without God as a proof of the goodness of its case. This new bravery, understood as the readiness to hold firm while gazing upon the abandonment of man, as the courage to endure fearful truth, as hardness against the inclination of man to deceive himself about his situation, is called probity.[12]

It is this probity, this "intellectual probity" that commands that all attempts to "mediate" between Enlightenment and Orthodoxy (those of the moderate Enlightenment as well as and especially those of the post-Enlightenment synthesis) be rejected, not just as inadequate but also and above all as lacking in probity. It compels the choice between Enlightenment and Orthodoxy and even commands abstention from the word "God" because it believes that the deepest lack of probity is to be found in the principles of the tradition itself.

Just because of its conscientiousness and morality, this atheism with a good, or even bad, conscience must be distinguished from the conscienceless atheism at which the past shuddered: Instead of wanting to live securely "under cover," the "Epicurean" who became an "idealist" during the persecutions of the sixteenth and seventeenth centuries learned to fight and die for honor and truth. Finally he became the "atheist" who rejected the belief in God out of conscience. With this it becomes clear that this atheism, compared not only with the original Epicureanism but also with the most "radical" atheism of the age of Enlightenment, is a descendant of the tradition grounded in the Bible; it concedes the thesis, the negation of the Enlightenment, on the grounds of an attitude the Bible alone made possible. Even though it denies that it is a "synthesis" of Enlightenment and Orthodoxy because it does not want to disguise its lack of faith in any way, it is still precisely the latest, most radical, and least contestable reconciliation of these opposing positions.

This atheism is the inheritor and judge of the belief in revelation, of the centuries-old, even millennial, conflict between belief and unbelief, of the ultimately short-lived but not therefore inconsequential romantic longing for lost belief, of Orthodoxy in its complex cunning. Fashioned out of gratitude, rebellion, longing, and indifference, it stands in simple probity. It claims to be capable of an original understanding of the human roots of the belief in God like no earlier philosophy, no philosophy at once less complex and less simple. The last word and final justification of the Enlightenment is atheism out of probity: Free from the polemical bitterness of the Enlightenment and the ambiguous reverence of Romanticism, it overcomes Orthodoxy radically by understanding it radically.

Thus the "truth" of the alternative of Orthodoxy or Enlightenment finally unveils itself as the alternative of Orthodoxy or atheism. Orthodoxy, looking with a hostile eye, knew this from the beginning. Now even the enemies of Orthodoxy no longer dispute it. For a Jew who cannot be orthodox and must hold unconditional political Zionism (the only possible "solution to the Jewish problem" on the basis of atheism) to be a highly honorable but in the long and serious run unsatisfactory answer, the situation created by that alternative, the contemporary situation, seems to allow no way out. This situation does not just appear to allow no way out, it really does not as long as one adheres firmly to modern presuppositions. If in the end there are only the alternatives of Orthodoxy or atheism, and if, correspondingly, the desirability of an enlightened Judaism cannot be rejected, then one is forced to question whether enlightenment must necessarily be modern enlightenment. Unless we can know in advance what cannot be known in advance, namely, that only new, unheard of, ultramodern thoughts can help us out of our predicament, we are obliged to approach the medieval Enlightenment for help—the Enlightenment of Maimonides.

But has not the Enlightenment of Maimonides been over-come long ago? Is it not the forerunner and model of precisely the moderate Enlightenment of the seventeenth and eighteenth centuries, which was least able to maintain itself? Indeed, is it not in some aspects even more "radical," even more dangerous to the spirit of Judaism than the modern Enlightenment itself? Does it not rest upon the unrestorable cosmology of Aristotle? Does it not stand or fall by such a questionable method of interpretation as allegoresis? Therefore, is not the modern Enlightenment, however questionable, nonetheless to be preferred to the medieval Enlightenment?

It would be punishable to pass over these or similar considerations. It would, however, only be possible to discuss them thoroughly, point by point, in the framework of an interpretation of Maimonides' *Guide of the Perplexed.* Instead, in what follows, we will attempt to direct attention to that guiding idea of the medieval Enlightenment that the modern Enlightenment and its heirs have lost. Through an understanding of that idea, many modern convictions and considerations lose their power: It is the idea of Law.

I

THE CONFLICT OF ANCIENTS AND MODERNS IN THE PHILOSOPHY OF JUDAISM:

Comments on Julius Guttmann's *Philosophies of Judaism*[1]

I

There is no investigation into the history of philosophy that is not at the same time a *philosophical* investigation. Without any doubt, a handbook of the history of the philosophy of Judaism that is based at every point on the most thorough knowledge of the sources as well as on previous research of them is desirable for scholarly research. This desideratum is so consummately fulfilled by Julius Guttmann's work, *Philosophies of Judaism*, that the understanding reader will initially take full satisfaction in allowing himself to be taught, in general and detail, by this outstanding expert, and will gratefully use this handbook, which in the past was always dispensed with and now is indispensable.

To be sure, the same understanding reader will notice promptly, if he does not know or assume it at the outset, that this desideratum of the scholarly enterprise would hardly by itself have led Guttmann to write his *Philosophies of Judaism*, even if added to it was the need to collect the findings of his own scholarship, hitherto scattered in numerous monographs and lecture notes. What concerns Guttman is the historical depiction of the philosophical problem that interests him most, namely, the problem of the "methodological distinctiveness of religion."[2]

In order not to misunderstand Guttmann's posing of the problem, one does well to recall his earlier text, *Religion und Wissenschaft im Mittelalterlichen und im Modernen Denken*. At the end of that text, explicitly drawing connections with *Kant* on the one hand and *Schleiermacher* on the other, he characterizes the task of the "philosophy of religion" as "the analysis of religious consciousness" in its "independence . . . vis-à-vis knowledge and morality."[3] More precisely, the philosophy of religion is "the demarcation of religion from all other realms of objects and consciousness, the elaboration of

The Conflict of Ancients and Moderns

23

the religious world proper and of its truth."[4] Thus determining the task of the "philosophy of religion," he seems to regard the task of philosophy in general as the understanding of *"culture,"* which divides itself into different "realms."

It is striking, however, that despite his unmistakable inclination to the philosophy of culture, Guttmann most studiously avoids the expressions "culture" or "domain of culture" and prefers instead the more formal and therefore less prejudicial expressions "domain of validity," "domain of truth," and "realm of objects and consciousness." Thus from the outset he arouses the suspicion that religion cannot be understood correctly in the framework of the concept of "culture." For the philosophy of culture understands "culture" as the "spontaneous generation" of the human spirit; however, religion, according to its own meaning, does not have this character.[5] Second, the other "domains of validity" may be conceived as "partial domains of truth," but religion raises the claim of universality.[6] Culture, which according to its own meaning rests on spontaneous generation, raises a claim to universality that appears to contradict the claim of religion to universality—religion that, according to its own meaning, was not generated by man but was *given* to him.

Guttmann does not go so far, to be sure. As we have already suggested, he believes that the "domain of validity" is the genus that embraces "culture" as well as religion. But, in any case, he sees himself compelled by the fact of religion as such (which just in this regard proves to be a crucial problem for the philosophy of culture) to maintain a noticeable distance from the philosophy of culture.[7]

Guttmann leaves no doubt that the "methodological distinctiveness of religion" is not an *original* problem.[8] One can flatly say that his whole history of the philosophy of Judaism has no other intention (or at least no other result) than proving that the "methodological" formulation of the question, in spite of or because of its not being original, offers the only guarantee for an appropriately scientific understanding of the Bible. As to its not being original, the "methodological" formulation of the question stems directly neither from religion (be it the Bible or the Talmud) nor from the collision of (biblical) religion and (Greek) philosophy. Rather, the only question that emerges directly from the collision is whether the teachings of revelation or the teachings of philosophy are *true*, particularly, for example, whether the world is created or eternal, whether providence extends to individuals or only to species, and whether the soul or only the intellect is immortal and the like. These are the questions with which medieval Jewish philosophy especially concerned itself and whose variegated treatments and answers Guttmann thoughtfully and thoroughly presents.

In place of the alternatives of Revelation or Reason, to be sure, there quickly, one might even say from the outset, appears the conciliating judgment that the teachings of Revelation are identical to the teachings of Reason. Thus at first "religion and philosophy are not divided *methodologically* but rather are reconciled *substantively*."[9] In this way, philosophy as well as religion suffer fundamental modifications. The problems of philosophy are "constituted and formed from the religious point of view," and thereby "the conceptions of ancient metaphysics" undergo "fundamental transformations" in the spirit of the "personalistic religiosity of the Bible."[10] On the other hand, there came about "a considerable transformation of biblical and talmudic Judaism,"[11] a more or less far-reaching surrender of the biblical conceptions of God, world, and man in favor of those of Greek philosophy.[12] The biblical conception could be more successfully defended in the element of philosophy only after medieval metaphysics, stemming from pagan antiquity, was replaced by the metaphysics of the Enlightenment, stemming directly from Christianity and indirectly from the Bible.[13] Of course, the ancient metaphysics that was authoritative for the Middle Ages was "teleological" and therefore "capable of being reconciled with revealed religion,"[14] whereas the "mechanistic transformation" of metaphysics in the modern time, especially in Spinoza, led to a necessary break with revealed religion.[15] But this loss is offset precisely because out of the *Bible's* spirit of "personalistic piety," the "inclination to a mechanistic concept of nature" and the revulsion against the assumption of purposeful forces, can, and in modernity actually does, come out as a "kind of polytheism."[16]

131,978

The Conflict of Ancients and Moderns

College of St. Francis Library
Joliet, Illinois

Even if the reconciliation between Judaism and philosophy achieved through *Mendelssohn* on the basis of the modern Enlightenment stands "more closely related to Jewish tradition" than the corresponding achievement of medieval neo-Platonists and Aristotelians,[17] one can still not remain content with it. This is not just because Mendelssohn, too, diverges in an essential point from the Jewish tradition[18] but also and above all because he holds firm to a presupposition of the whole Jewish tradition that is already shaky in his case: the idea of a revealed, given religion. Mendelssohn denies that communication of the truths of Reason by Revelation is possible. Thus for him who especially allows no superrational truths of faith, Revelation can only remain in a very limited sense. Indeed, "no place is left for the truth of historical revelation."[19] Thus, while Mendelssohn better preserves the Bible's *content* than his medieval predecessors, he no longer can give as satisfying an account of its *form*, of its character as Revelation.

This fact already arouses the suspicion that, if one wants to preserve the Bible's content in the element of philosophy *entirely*, one must sacrifice the traditional concept of its form, i.e., the belief in its Revelation. The Bible may no longer be understood as revealed but rather as produced by religious consciousness. And the task of the "philosophy of religion" no longer consists of reconciling the teachings of Revelation and Reason but rather in analysis of the religious consciousness. Therefore, Guttmann especially, who views the actual task of the "philosophy of religion" as determining the "methodological distinctiveness of religion," must have sacrificed the belief in Revelation in advance.[20] The history of the philosophy of Judaism as a whole thus produces the teaching that, because of the failure of the outwardly so much more imposing "substantive" and "metaphysical" attempts at a solution, the outwardly so unimposing "formal" and "methodological" way of thinking has proved to be *the* condition of the possibility of an appropriately scientific understanding of the Bible.

The extraordinary fascination of Guttmann's reasoning for the superiority of modern philosophy over medieval (and this reasoning is the spiritual bond that holds together his very careful and extensive individual analyses) cannot be disputed.

Guttmann himself points to the obvious objection to which his reasoning is nevertheless exposed, when he says:

> Though the medieval thinkers are rooted as total personalities more strongly in Jewish tradition and substance of life, and though the belief in the divine authority of revelation is more self-evident to them, nonetheless, in their theoretical interpretation of Judaism, the modern thinkers hold firm, with greater powers of resistance, to the original sense of its central religious thoughts.[21]

This conclusion allows the interpretation that appropriate scientific knowledge of Judaism is purchased at the price of belief in the authority of Revelation and of a considerable loss of Jewish "substance of life." Stated fundamentally, it is that the owl of Minerva begins its flight at dusk. Still, Guttmann does not think so fatalistically, so hopelessly. His opinion is rather that the scientific knowledge of Judaism is precisely an act of the self-assertion of Judaism. Judaism is endangered in the modern world and by the modern world as never before— granted. Its scientific self-knowledge is, however, not so much a symptom of its disease as the most suitable means for its relief or even its cure. The danger Judaism has fallen into by the victory of reflection over the original cannot be overcome by means of a fictitious retreat behind reflection but rather only by decisively carrying out reflection itself. By now it is only the least original, least naive formulation of the question that is suited to uphold the original in that it teaches one *to understand* it.

The result that Guttmann arrives at can thus also be interpreted in a wholly opposite way. If Guttmann's thesis, as we have understood it, corresponded to the facts, one would have to come to terms with this awkward circumstance. But have we understood it correctly? We understood Guttmann to mean that modern Judaism, which stands far less firmly on its legs, disposes of an essentially more appropriate philosophical understanding of the content of Jewish tradition than a much more vital medieval Judaism. As we have shown, this opinion is ambiguous. However, it is not just ambiguous but also paradoxical, because it postulates a paradoxical disproportion between life and thought. This disproportion may strike the modern way of thinking as simply obvious, but it cannot be denied that it is nevertheless questionable. Thus we ask: Does Guttmann really mean that modern, more than medieval, philosophy gives Judaism the opportunity to preserve the content of its tradition, while understanding it, even if at the sacrifice of the belief in Revelation?

II

Guttmann concludes his history of the philosophy of Judaism with a critical presentation of the work of Hermann *Cohen*. Insofar as "the great achievement of Herman Cohen"[22] is the most perfect form in which modern Jewish thought has expressed itself, in it the barrier that separates modern thought from Judaism must be most clearly recognizable. Guttmann's objection to Cohen is that Cohen no longer has the possibility of "affirming in its absolute reality" the existence of God. On the basis of Cohen's presuppositions, the existence of God, too, "must find [its] logical place in the fixed postulates of consciousness."[23] Even in his last period, when essentially he stood closer to Judaism than in the earlier ones, "the methodological bases of his system restrain him from the possibility of interpreting God as a Reality. . . ."[24] This incapacity is, moreover, all the more astonishing because the content of Judaism is validated in Cohen much more than in Mendelssohn, and especially more in Cohen than in the medieval philosophers.

The incapacity "to interpret God as a Reality" by no means distinguishes Cohen alone. In the programmatic comments at the end of his earlier work, *Religion und Wissenschaft*, Guttmann decisively insists that the "philosophy of religion" may not just concern itself with "religious experience" but must also give an account of the "objective side" of this experience and also, and above all, of the "character of reality of religious things."[25] This assertion bears witness that the understanding—even the recognition of this "character of reality"—is the characteristic embarrassment for the modern "philosophy of religion" inaugurated by Schleiermacher.

Modern "philosophy of religion" is distinguished from the earlier kind in that it no longer has its foundation in metaphysics but in epistemology.[26] This means that modern philosophy no longer (indeed, less than ever) understands man as a member of the cosmos, as a natural being (even if an outstanding one) among other natural beings. Rather, and oppositely, it understands nature from man, or, more precisely, from consciousness as that which constitutes nature. Just for that reason, it cannot "discover" God as the *Creator* from the cosmos, but rather only from consciousness. Under the sway of the cosmological orientation—despite or because of all the difficulties concentrated in the problem of "analogy"—the "Reality," the "absolute actuality" of God, was self-evident; hence just this reality becomes fundamentally incomprehensible once the modern orientation has fully established itself. The embarrassment gets no smaller, but even greater, when "consciousness" is replaced by "existence," by "man."

But what is the philosophy of existence doing in these comments on Guttmann's *Philosophies of Judaism*, when Guttmann does not devote one word to it, even its Jewish form, unless in that terse reference to the "metaphysical and irrationalistic tendencies that generally rule the thought of the time"?[27] But might he not have had it in mind, even if he does not speak of it extensively or even explicitly? And is that terse reference to the philosophy of existence not rather a terse dispatch of it? We will try to develop somewhat more extensively in Guttmann's sense what he meant and hinted at by following the road signs he erected in his critique of Cohen.

We had said that the embarrassment in which modern thought finds itself gets not smaller but greater, when "consciousness" is replaced by "existence," by "man." For it is first on the basis of this advance that the basic cosmological distinction, "Eternal-Mutable" (decisive for the older philosophy but transcended by the basic theological distinction, "God—the Created," and made questionable by the basic modern distinction, "Spirit-Nature") becomes fully obsolete. If it now comes to the basic distinction of man-nature, and it is conformably asserted that the existence of God can be understood not from nature but rather only from man, then the only guarantee is lost that God's existence will not be wholly "internalized" and thus evaporate. An unfailing sign for this is that the teaching of the Creation as the Creation of non-human nature as well is even more of an embarrassment for the philosophy of existence than for idealistic philosophy. This is shown most plainly in the case of Friedrich Gogarten, who has fought idealistic philosophy on the basis of the philosophy of existence perhaps more decisively than all others. To be sure, Gogarten too says that "the Creation is full and overfull of the gifts and works of God," but he continues:

> The works of God, in which God's Being-for-us and, correspondingly, our Being-of-God come to light, in which, that is, He reveals Himself as our Creator, in which "the Good" is at once both God's gift and God's demand, these works of God subsist in this, that we men are respectively from each other, what we are and who we are. This Being-from (is) the original Being of man, and therefore it is man's peculiar Being. As such it may not be understood as causal Being, like, to be sure, the Being of things, the Being in living and unliving nature.[28]

One sees that here it remains wholly obscure whether the "causal Being" of the natural things also must be understood as created Being. In a newer publication, Gogarten indeed retains the ambiguous mention of "causal Being." He even cites a passage from Luther's interpretation of Genesis in which, of course, *all* creatures are included, and thereby appropriates for himself the assertion of Creation in its original sense. But in his own expressions, he just as studiously passes over the createdness of non-human nature. He thus says: ". . . there, where the law is fulfilled in its full sense, *Creation* too (becomes) plain, revealed. It is revealed in how God created man. . . ."[29] We believe we do Gogarten no injustice when we say that except to the extent that the theological tradition draws him belatedly into its spell, Creation has meaning for him only as the creation of man. And insofar as Gogarten may count as the representative of the philosophy of existence, we may further say that the philosophy of existence is even less able than idealistic philosophy to understand the teaching of Creation in its original, biblical sense.

After all, just like the philosophy of existence, idealistic philosophy had also torn nature and man asunder (under the headings of the "Is" and the "Ought" and, correspondingly, "nature" and "morality"). Thanks to its connection with Kant, however, idealistic philosophy had preserved the most distinct memory that the "idea of Creation," even if it "does not (claim to) provide a theoretical explanation for the origin of the universe," still concerns, also and in the first instance, "the relationship between God and the world," the relationship between God and non-human nature.[30] Above all others, not only did Cohen not leave in obscurity the fact that the idea of God (itself admittedly only comprehensible from the basis of moral consciousness) has a necessary relation to the "causal Being" of nature,[31] but also he even made it the starting point of his theological discussion. Idealistic philosophy thus shows itself superior to the philosophy of existence in one, not to say *the*, decisive point; it is superior by remembering the original sense of the teaching of Creation.

The fact that Cohen admittedly only remembered and no longer believed this teaching is shown not only by his incapacity, as demonstrated by Guttmann, "to conceive God as Reality"; it is shown even more directly by his answer to the objection of an Orthodox Jew to his theology. To the objection "and what of the בורא עולם", Cohen knew no other reply than—to weep and thus to confess that the cleft between his faith and the faith of the tradition is unbridgeable.[32] We do not doubt—indeed, since there was no reticence about assuring us of it openly, we even know—that the philosophers of existence could not have fallen into this embarrassment for an answer: so lost has been even the memory of the original sense of the teaching of Creation.

If, then, Cohen's idealistic philosophy at least shows itself superior to the philosophy of existence in this decisive point, no one correspondingly will dispute that for the rest, the philosophy of existence grasps the "existential" sense of the Bible more securely than idealistic philosophy. But just in this superiority of the philosophy of existence over idealistic philosophy, the corresponding superiority of idealistic philosophy over medieval philosophy merely repeats itself. Just thereby it becomes clear that substituting the philosophy of existence for idealistic philosophy does not represent a radical break but only an advance. In this substitution, too, Guttmann's law, posited with respect to the substitution of idealistic for cosmological philosophy, proves itself. Progress in the "theoretical interpretation" of the Bible has been bought at the price of a considerable loss in the "living substance" of revealed religion.

And thus, since idealistic philosophy and the philosophy of existence belong together, we may summarize. Under the sway of the cosmological orientation, the danger existed that, while faith in the existence of God as the Creator, and also and especially of nature, remained wholly unbroken, the content of Revelation would be misinterpreted in the sense of Greek "humanism." After the surrender of the cosmological orientation, the opposite danger existed. With the understanding preservation of the "existential" sense of the Bible, not only is faith in Revelation surrendered, as it first seemed, but also faith in the Creation.[33] Therefore not "only" faith in Revelation has been endangered by modern philosophy.

It is clear now that we have misunderstood Guttmann considerably. His critique of Cohen shows that he claims not *the* but only a *certain* superiority of modern philosophy over medieval. In truth, his thesis holds that modern philosophy is more capable than medieval to preserve understandingly the *"inner world"* of faith. But it is less capable than the latter of recognizing the essential relationship to "outer" *nature* of this God, who rules the "inner world." Under these circumstances, the least one can ask is that modern and medieval philosophy must supplement each other in some way.

Guttman's unusually energetic interest in Jewish medieval philosophy is to be understood radically only on the basis of this requirement. It is thus no accident that of the approximately 360 pages of text of *Philosophies of Judaism*, 245 pages are devoted solely to Jewish medieval philosophy.[34] One would mistake Guttmann's philosophical impulse entirely if one saw in this numerical ratio exclusively the reflection of the quantitative relationship of medieval to late ancient and modern Jewish philosophical literature, or the reflection of the relation

of their historical effects, or if one wished to believe that Guttmann only brings such great interest to medieval philosophy
in order to show how splendidly far we have come. Guttmann
knows too well that we have every reason to attend the school
of the medieval philosophers. That is why, finally, he ab-
stained from a discussion of the philosophy of existence. He
does not deceive himself about the fact that our contemporary
embarrassment cannot be put to an end by the *natural progress*
from idealistic philosophy to a *"new* thinking"; rather, it is
much more likely that the *forcible retreat* from the newest
thinking to *old* thinking can. And even if he grants a certain
superiority to modern over medieval philosophy, he makes even
this admission only insofar as modern philosophy, more than
medieval, makes valid the "central religious thoughts" of the
Jewish tradition. Just thereby he recognizes the Jewish tradition, and thus an unmodern, premodern instance, as judge over
modern thought, so announcing most visibly his insight into
the fundamental inadequacy of modern thought.

III

As it has turned out, Guttmann asserts not *the* but only a
certain superiority of modern Jewish philosophy over medieval. Now even this qualified assertion (which we ask to be
understood as made precise earlier) has as its presupposition
that faith in Revelation does not belong to those "central religious thoughts" of Judaism, whose preservation in the element of reflection has been purchased at the price of renunciation of faith in Revelation. But does this faith not *necessarily*
belong to the "central religious thoughts" of Judaism? Indeed,
not just as one indispensable element among others but rather
the condition of the possibility of all of them? Do these thoughts
remain the same, or do they not most fundamentally change
their meaning, if one no longer understands them as God-given
but rather as produced out of man's "religious consciousness,"
be it "before God?" If, on the other hand, Judaism is *essentially*
a "monotheistic revealed religion,"[35] then medieval philosophy stands incomparably closer to Judaism than modern phi-

losophy. For at least "the formal recognition of the authority of Revelation is a self-evident presupposition for even the most radical thinkers of the Jewish Middle Ages insofar as they want to stay Jews."[36] In view of this powerful, decisive advantage, in the fundamental comparison of medieval and modern philosophy one can in good conscience neglect the fact, undoubtedly correctly brought forth by Guttmann that important "religious thoughts" of Judaism have in general been more clearly and surely conceived by the moderns than by their predecessors.

For which "central religious thoughts" are actually more clearly and surely conceived by the moderns than by their predecessors, and by what path did the moderns come to this advantage? These thoughts are nothing other than the center of the biblical religion. "The distinctiveness of biblical religion," however, "is due to the ethical personalism of its consciousness of God."[37] These thoughts are secured by the moderns, not exegetically, not theologically, but through the analysis of "religious consciousness," an analysis inaugurated by the "epoch-making" achievement of Schleiermacher.[38] Now the "personalist character of biblical religion put it into thoroughgoing opposition to the other type of spiritual and universal religion, which, with all the differences of their essences, lies at the common ground of mysticism and pantheism."[39] It is on the basis of this typology, whose modern origins are marked on its forehead, that Guttmann proves modern philosophy's superiority over medieval philosophy. For, according to his assertion, the medieval philosophers are inferior to the moderns just because they reinterpret the biblical religion in the sense of the diametrically opposed religion "of mysticism or contemplation."[40]

If, however, it now finally turns out that the idea of an analysis of "religious consciousness" is *the* condition for the possibility of an understanding preservation of the biblical "type of piety," one cannot avoid this question. In orientation to what "type of piety" was this idea actually conceived originally? Guttmann's answer is unambiguous. "In its decisive elements," Schleiermacher's "characterization of religion accords with the descriptions of the religious experience that are often given in the literature of *mysticism* and its corresponding concept of religion."[41] Even though "later research has distanced itself far from [Schleiermacher's] views in the interpretation of the content of religion, even though more recent research has also and especially attacked the analysis of the characteristically biblical "type of piety," nonetheless, Schleiermacher "has determined the process of their work."[42] Now Guttmann, who sees in the determination of the *"methodological* distinctiveness of religion" the task of the "philosophy of religion," is the last one who needs to be taught that a "process" is never an impartial, unprejudiced technique but always decides in advance about the possible content. Therefore, out of the insight into the genesis of the modern method of the analysis of "religious consciousness," there grows a *suspicion*, which of course at first is *only* a suspicion. Does the modern method, which leads to surer recognition of the biblical "type of piety" than the medieval method, only allow a subsequent correction with respect to the concept of religion achieved from the perspective of "mysticism," in just the same way that medieval philosophy could only subsequently make valid the concept of God and the "inner attitude" of biblical religion, only within the framework of a predetermined Aristotelian, or rather Platonic, way of thinking? In other words, we harbor a suspicion difficult to quiet, namely, that the same thing occurs in modern as in medieval philosophy—the betrayal of the biblical inheritance for the sake of an alien "piety."

Indeed, the betrayal committed by modern philosophy seems much worse to us than the offense of earlier philosophy. This is so not only because the moderns are unambiguously instructed by a modern example, namely, their own historical research, and thus do knowingly what the earlier ones did by oversight and not only because they have surrendered the belief in Revelation, which was a "self-evident presupposition" for their predecessors. Rather, above all, it is because the moderns commit their betrayal in a much more concealed way and therefore in a much more "substance"-destroying way. So at least, someone who recognizes the Jewish tradition as the judge of modern thought would have to deem.

The Conflict of Ancients and Moderns

However one must or may wish to decide our *querelle des anciens et des modernes*, it is established that, in contrast to modern philosophy, not only is the recognition of the authority of Revelation a "self-evident presupposition" for medieval philosophy but also that the "philosophical justification" of this recognition is an essential concern. Guttmann goes further; according to his assertion, the "philosophy of religion" is even *the* original achievement of the Middle Ages.[43]

> The original achievement of the Middle Ages is having made religion into a problem of philosophy. Otherwise wholly dependent on the ancient traditions and productive only in working through and developing further traditional motifs of thought, medieval thought here opened up a new area of problems and introduced a new motif to the philosophical consciousness.[44]

Guttmann's assertion that the "philosophy of religion" is *the* achievement of medieval philosophy is open to certain objections at first sight.[45] Admittedly, the assertion itself seems less vulnerable to us than the presuppositions on whose basis it achieves its characteristic evidence. Since, as we have seen, Guttmann only assumes a certain superiority of medieval over modern philosophy,[46] he does not see himself forced into a radical critique of the basic modern concepts. In particular, he is therefore free to proceed in his study of the Middle Ages from modern categories of philosophy. If one bases oneself on the categorization of philosophy into, say, epistemology, logic, ethics, aesthetics, and philosophy of religion, and if one thus presupposes, for example, that the problems of natural theology and rational psychology are to be treated within the philosophy of religion (it is in this sense that Guttmann designates Mendelssohn's *Phaedo* and *Morgenstunden* as his "major works of the philosophy of religion"[47]), one then must indeed necessarily seek the originality of medieval philosophy solely or primarily in the philosophy of religion. No further elaboration is needed to show that one would reach another verdict if one based oneself on the ancient categorization of philosophy (surely more appropriate for the study of the older philosophy) into logic, physics, metaphysics, ethics, and politics, and further, that it is not a merely technical question whether one must characterize a problem as "metaphysical" or "religious-philosophical."

Despite the questionableness of its presuppositions, the assertion that the "philosophy of religion" is *the* original achievement of medieval thought is eminently arguable. One must only provide it with the limitations Guttmann has himself taken up. Guttmann in no way denies but rather he explicitly asserts that medieval philosophy has [taken up] "fundamental transformations" of ancient metaphysics.[48] But in Guttmann's opinion, in doing so it only gave non-ancient answers to ancient questions; it did not modify the questions essentially. The only non-ancient *question* that medieval philosophy posed is the question of the meaning and the possibility of Revelation and of its relation to reason. Guttmann denies just as little that the "fundamental transformations" of ancient philosophy,[49] completed by the philosophy of the Middle Ages, made historically possible the break with the ancient mode of thought that was completed by modern philosophy. Thus medieval philosophy concerns us not only because of its "philosophy of religion." But this transformation of ancient philosophy in the Middle Ages was not completed so much out of philosophical intent as out of the urge to adapt "the world picture of ancient metaphysics to the personalistic religion of the Bible."[50] Thus the discussion about Guttmann's assertion that *the* original achievement of medieval thought is the "philosophy of religion" threatens to become boundless. It is thus time that we abstain from removing this assertion from the only context within which it gains a clear meaning.

Guttmann obviously does not mean by his assertion that the contemporary historian, who proceeds from contemporary formulations of the question, is interested in medieval philosophy above all for its "philosophy of religion." Rather, he is of the opinion that for medieval philosophy itself, which is just thereby characteristically distinguished from both ancient and modern philosophy, the "philosophy of religion" as the "peculiar task"[51] stands at the midpoint, or, to speak more precisely, at the beginning, as the primary task. For the religion with which medieval philosophy deals is revealed religion. Insofar as Revelation is *constitutive* for this philosophy, the problem posed by Revelation is *the* problem of medieval philosophy. Through the reality of Revelation, the situation of philosophy has changed *through and through*. We can wish for no more authoritative witness for this fact than *Maimonides*.

Alexander of Aphrodisias adduced three reasons for the differences of opinion in philosophy and thus for the difficulties of philosophizing. Maimonides sees himself required to add a fourth. This new reason distinguishes itself *essentially* from the preceding three. For those three reasons concern the *natural* difficulties of philosophizing, whereas the reason added by Maimonides is *historical*. Maimonides says:

> However, *in our times* there is a fourth cause that he did not mention because it did not exist among them. It is habit and upbringing. . . . In a similar way, man has love for, and the wish to defend, opinions to which he is habituated and in which he has been brought up and has a feeling of repulsion for opinions other than those. For this reason also man is blind to the apprehension of the true realities and inclines toward the things to which he is habituated. This happened to the multitude with regard to the belief in His corporeality. . . . All this is due to people being habituated to, and brought up on, *texts* that it is an established usage to think highly of and to regard as true and whose external meaning is indicative of the corporeality of God. . . .[52]

Now the Greeks were surely not lacking in texts that seemed, and not only *seemed*, to teach the corporeality of God. These writings did not hinder Greek philosophy because they were not authoritative. Thus it is not habituation to texts as such, the rule of tradition as such, but the habituation to texts of unconditional authority and the rule of a tradition of unconditional authority that make philosophizing especially difficult. The fact that a tradition based on Revelation has broken into the world of philosophy has augmented the *natural* difficulties of philosophizing, which are entailed by man's "cave" existence, by the *historical* difficulty.[53]

One can express oneself about the situation of philosophy under the rule of Revelation in as *enlightened* a way as Maimonides or as *gratefully* as the otherwise "more enlightened"

Rabbi Levi ben Gerson, who recognizes in Revelation "a wonderful guidance for rational research."[54] In any case, medieval philosophy is distinguished from ancient as well as modern philosophy by the situation entailed by the reality of Revelation. Every medieval philosopher must explicitly or at least silently, frankly or at least outwardly, take *account* of Revelation in the treatment of all important questions. Even more, for all medieval philosophers, "insofar as they wish to remain Jews," at least "the formal acknowledgement of the authority of Revelation" is "a self-evident *presupposition.*"[55] This sentence should be understood quite literally. First it means that there may be dispute about what counts as the *content* of Revelation. There may thus be dispute about the createdness or eternity of matter, about the immortality of the soul, or only of the intellect, about the eternal duration or the future destruction of the present world, and so forth. But no dispute is possible about the reality of Revelation and about the duty to obey it. Further, it means that the acknowledgment of the authority of Revelation is "*self-evident.*"[56] To be sure, the medieval philosophers do make an effort to set forth the possibility of Revelation philosophically and the reality of Revelation historically. But these substantiations only confirm what was already determined *before* substantiation, what was understood "by itself." For the possibility of Revelation follows from its reality; its reality, however, is known immediately. Despite and because of the mediating tradition, it is known immediately. In the superhuman wisdom and justice of the Torah the seeing Jew *sees*, and in the superhuman beauty of the Koran the seeing Muslim *sees*, that Revelation is real.

Finally, Guttmann's cited sentence means that the acknowledgment of the authority of Revelation is the *presupposition* of philosophizing as such. This presupposition precedes all philosophizing. It is not posited as a basis for human thought but is imposed on human thought in advance. Because the acknowledgment of the authority of Revelation is *prior* to philosophizing, and because Revelation claims man *wholly*, philosophizing now only becomes possible as *commanded* by the revealed law. Thus it is no longer at the discretion of the man who is suited to philosophizing whether he wants to phi-

losophize or not, as though he had to bear the natural consequence of his discretion and nothing more. Now whether the
philosopher is appointed to philosophize by himself or by an
authority (cf. Plato, *Apology*, 28d) is no longer undetermined,
and a god no longer summons one to philosophizing by a dark,
enigmatic, multiple admonition (cf. Plato, *Apology*, 21a–b, and
Phaedo, 60e–61a). Rather, the one and only God obliges the
men who are suited for it to philosophize, through a manifest,
unambiguous, simple command of His revealed Law.[57] Even
and precisely the "most radical thinkers" of the Middle Ages,
above all Averroes himself, teach this. The new *situation* of
philosophizing, being bound *through* Revelation, thus results
in a new *task* for philosophers, their responsibility *before* Revelation. Their "exoteric" writings have the function not so
much of "persuading" or "inciting" men to philosophizing but
rather by means of a *"legal speculation"* of showing that philosophizing is a duty, and that in its form and its content it
corresponds to the opinion of Revelation.[58]

In this sense, we appropriate entirely for ourselves Guttmann's assertion that *the* original achievement of the Middle
Ages was the "philosophy of religion." Medieval (Islamic and
Jewish) philosophy characteristically distinguished itself from
ancient as well as modern philosophy in this. Understanding
itself as bound and authorized by Revelation, it sees its first
and most urgent concern as laying the foundations of philosophy in a *legal grounding of philosophy*.

With this conclusion we have also gained a first indication
of how medieval philosophers understand religion. They do
not understand it as a "domain of validity" or as a "direction
of consciousness," and least of all as a "domain of culture,"
but rather, as *Law*.

IV

The first and fundamental task of medieval philosophy is the
legal grounding of philosophy. Above all, this is the demonstration that those men who are suited to philosophizing are
obligated and thus authorized to philosophize by the revealed

Law. At the same time, the legal grounding of philosophy assures that the philosophizing that is authorized by the Law enjoys complete freedom, that it is just or almost as free as if it stood under no law. This philosophizing, authorized and liberated in this way, takes Revelation, like every other existing thing, for its theme. The *philosophical grounding of the Law* that comes about in this way distinguishes itself from the legal grounding of philosophy in that the latter, as the foundation of philosophy, precedes all philosophizing, while the former is a part of the structure of philosophical teachings itself. Revelation, *before* which philosophy is as such accountable, is thus *for* philosophy only *one* theme among others. And indeed, it is in no way the first or central theme. Rather, logic stands in the first place and metaphysics in the center. We do not exactly—at least not exactly yet—want to assert that Revelation is the last theme of medieval philosophy. We content ourselves with the repeated conclusion that it is one theme among others. While the legal grounding of philosophy is its foundation, the philosophical grounding of the Law is a part, and not even the central part, of the structure of philosophical teachings.

But in the philosophical grounding of the Law, the presupposition of philosophizing itself comes under discussion and in such a manner that in a certain way it becomes questionable. In any case, it is *only* treated philosophically in the philosophical grounding of the Law, since it is treated exclusively legally in the legal grounding of philosophy. Therefore, the philosophical grounding of the Law is the place in the structure of teachings of medieval philosophy in which the presupposition of (medieval) philosophizing becomes the theme of philosophy. One may therefore characterize the philosophical grounding of the Law precisely as the philosophical grounding of medieval philosophy. How then does it happen that the philosophical grounding is nevertheless only a secondary theme of medieval philosophy? We may now confidently assert that the central task for the interpretation of medieval philosophy is answering this question. One cannot, however, answer this question, one cannot even render it precise in the requisite way, if one has not already understood the philosophical grounding of the Law given by the medieval philosophers. We thus turn to Guttmann with the question: What does the teaching of the medieval "philosophy of religion" say? And indeed, we only need occupy ourselves with the "philosophy of religion" of the "rationalist tendency." For, first of all, "an unlimited rationalism" rules far and wide "in Arabic and Jewish philosophy."[59] It "was dominant" especially in Jewish philosophy.[60] Second, and above all, the unbelieving philosophical fundament of the medieval belief in Revelation must stand out most clearly precisely in "Revelation-believing rationalism."

As for the "philosophy of religion" of the medieval Jewish rationalists, it deserves Guttmann's depiction of it as rationalistic, just as much and perhaps even more than does the "philosophy of religion" of modern "Revelation-believing rationalism." It is not just that these medieval thinkers secure the reality of Revelation through what is intended as a strict historical proof, so that for them "the belief in Revelation has the certitude of natural knowledge."[61] Rather, above all, they deny that any excess of the content of Revelation exists beyond the realm of reason. According to Saadia, whose doctrine was "accepted by most succeeding Jewish philosophers," the content of "divine Revelation is identical . . . to the content of reason. Negatively, this means that there is no contradiction between the two spheres; positively, it signifies that through its own powers reason is capable of reaching the content of the divine truth. This holds equally for the theoretical as for the moral content of Revelation."[62] If reason can recognize by itself all theoretical and practical truths, then, indeed, an "inevitable" question is: "What is the purpose of a revelation of truths, if reason can apprehend them by its own powers?" The classic answer to this question holds that Revelation has a "pedagogic" purpose. "In the first place, Revelation seeks to make the truth available to every man, even to those who are unable to think for themselves. Second, it seeks to protect the philosophers themselves from the uncertainties and inconsistencies of thought, and to give them from the very beginning that absolute truth at which their thought would arrive only after sustained and protracted effort." This conception of the purpose of Revelation and of the relation of Revelation to reason ruled for centuries. "Even the Enlightenment of the eighteenth century, insofar as it maintains the belief in Revelation, grasps the relationship between reason and Revelation in fundamentally the same manner."[63]

However fundamental the agreement may be between medieval and modern "Revelation-believing rationalism," a no less fundamental difference persists between them. "The religion of reason of the Middle Ages is distinguished . . . from the natural religion of the Enlightenment in this: its sole vehicle is philosophical knowledge."[64] This means that, while for the modern Enlightenment the truths of Revelation are at the same time the truths of a "healthy common sense," and thus are accessible to all men without further ado, according to the teaching of the medieval rationalists, only the philosophers can recognize the truths of Revelation by themselves and even they can do so only after strenuous, protracted preparations. If, then, according to the teaching of the modern Enlightenment, Revelation actually has nothing to reveal, and if therefore this Enlightenment's belief in Revelation merits the destructive, contemptuous critique to which Lessing subjected it,[65] medieval "Revelation-believing rationalism" does not, at least as it appears at first sight, seem open to criticism and contemptible in the same way.

According to the teaching of medieval rationalism, Revelation thus has an understandable "pedagogic" purpose. It fulfills this purpose also and precisely in the philosopher. It offers him, as it were, the tenets whose proof is the independent accomplishment of a reason incited by the communication of the tenets. In order to be able to fulfill this purpose, Revelation would, however, have to offer these tenets unambiguously. But that is out of the question, because reason alone decides what the teaching of Revelation is, since reason alone can interpret Revelation.[66] Thus the value of Revelation for philosophy becomes questionable. In any case, Revelation is indispensable only for the many, who are incapable of knowing even the few truths necessary for them—truths, by the way, communicated by the literal meaning of Revelation. Along with this purpose of popular pedagogy, Revelation has the additional but just as philosophically irrelevant function of supplementing the rational "ethical commandments" through "norms of right of a purely technical kind."[67] This according to Guttmann.

We must confess that "Revelation-believing rationalism" understood this way is not only factually untenable (it is that in Guttmann's view as well [68]) but above all it seems incomprehensible in itself. We admit that even he who believes that Revelation tells the philosopher nothing that he cannot tell himself can still "believe" in Revelation. That is, he can take note that a primary source of Revelation exists and that all the insights he has won independently find themselves, even if more or less concealed, in this primary source. But since he could not *rediscover* them in this primary source if he had not *first* discovered them along the route of his own reflection, what *interest* does he then have in Revelation? Certainly the many are dependent on Revelation, but what do the many concern the philosopher? In particular, what do the many concern the haughty Islamic and Jewish Aristotelians of the Middle Ages? What is utterly incomprehensible, what is outrageously incomprehensible about this "Revelation-believing rationalism" is that it "believes" in Revelation because Revelation is demonstrated to it as a historical fact, although no serious interest, no passionate dependency, drives it to Revelation. The fact of Revelation so understood is a *factum brutum* that, like all *facta bruta*, may be "interesting" to curious fact and cause chasers but just because of that does not concern the philosopher. Whoever thus "believes" in Revelation, really retains, as Lessing says, only the name and rejects the substance.

There can only be an *interest* in Revelation if one *needs* it. The philosopher needs Revelation if he knows that his capacity for knowledge is in principle inadequate to know *the* truth. The conviction of the inadequacy of human reason to know *the* truth, i.e., the decisively important truth, is the condition of possibility for a philosopher's having an interest as a philosopher in Revelation. The classic of Jewish rationalism in the Middle Ages, Maimonides, is imbued with this conviction. The decisively important teaching, the teaching upon whose truth the possibility of being a Jew depends absolutely, namely, the teaching of the createdness of the world, according to Maimonides' express and emphatic explanation is not subject to proof. Science can, to be sure (and that is already a lot), weaken the arguments of the unbelieving philosophers for the eternity of the world. More than that, it can make the creation of the world probable, but it cannot prove it. In the end, therefore, science must leave the question unanswered and accept the answer offered by Revelation.[69]

Philosophy is thus undoubtedly *dependent* on Revelation. Maimonides is not satisfied to determine this dependency; he strives for a fundamental understanding of it. According to Maimonides' teaching, man can know only *his* world, the "lower world," the world under the heavens, the world that surrounds him, lies before his eyes and is known to him. His knowledge of the "upper world," of the heavens, of that which is "above nature," his knowledge of "God and the angels," necessarily remains fragmentary and doubtful. The "lower world" is the world of becoming and decay. The ground of all becoming and decay is matter. Matter, our determination by it and our dependence on it, is the reason we can only inadequately fulfill our highest and actual calling, the knowledge of "God and the Angels." The highest knowledge for us consists of secrets; only occasionally does the truth shine forth for us so that we are of the opinion that it is day. Just as quickly, however, truth is removed again from our sight by matter and our matter-confined life. We live in a deep, dark night, which is only occasionally illuminated by lightning bolts. Thus, because man's understanding has a necessary limit, given with human nature, man is obligated, for the sake of his Lord's honor, to stop at this limit and to subject himself to the teachings of Revelation, which he cannot understand or prove.[70] Revelation, however, is communicated to man exclusively by prophets, i.e. by men who dispose of a direct knowledge of the "upper world," which is essentially inaccessible to the philosopher.[71] Thus, even and precisely, the philosopher needs direction through Revelation.

If one understands Maimonides' "Revelation-believing rationalism" in the way just sketched out, it not only becomes understandable in itself but further, it also escapes the criticism Guttmann directs against it in order to find a motive for the departure from this medieval position to the fundamental modern distinction between the theoretical and the religious consciousness of truth. According to his assertion, the "Revelation-believing rationalism" of the Middle Ages necessarily leads to the reputed teaching of double truth. In that teaching, for the first time the problem appears of how the independence of the religious consciousness from the scientific consciousness and vice-versa are "to be protected and at the same time bound up into a unified consciousness of truth." For

> if the authorities of Revelation and metaphysical knowledge are maintained side by side as equally, absolutely valid cases of truth, when there are differences between them, there is no possibility of a principled arrangement and there remains only the path of mutual accommodation from instance to instance. The protest against this procedure of accommodation, with its artificialities and violence, is the inner motive of the thought of double truth.[72]

We would venture the opinion that that "principled arrangement," which is precisely what Guttmann finds missing, was in fact achieved by Maimonides. We do not want to say thereby that his "accommodations" of Revelation and reason must be satisfying in every case and that one might not be allowed in particular, perhaps, to reflect on the interpretation of the Bible in the sense of Aristotelian cosmology, made possible by allegoresis, and the like. In any case, the arrangement suggested by Maimonides is principled insofar as through it the *instance* is determined that must settle the conflict between reason and Revelation. This instance (self-evident for a rationalist) is reason. Maimonides *proves* that reason has a limit and that it must thus accept the suprarational teachings of Revelation, without being able to understand and hence to prove them.

Maimonides' rational critique of reason shows that philosophy only actually knows the "lower world," and that, rising therefrom, it can prove the existence, unity, and incorporeality of God. Contemplative knowledge of the "upper world" is only possible for the prophets and is thus denied to the philosophers. Now it is through the prophets that the transcendant truth of philosophy is made known to the philosophers as to all men: that the world is not eternal but created. And this truth is distinguished in principle by the fact that it is absolutely necessary for life. For though the possibility of Revelation as such does not depend on the truth of the teaching of Creation, yet the truth and the possible absoluteness of one particular revelation do.[73] Thus for man, on the whole, all truth necessary for his life is accessible through reason *and* Revelation. Through reason he essentially becomes aware of *his* world and its dependence upon the "upper world" he cannot reach. Through Revelation he learns of those truths that transcend rational knowledge and that he needs for his life. Now, to be sure, Revelation not only imparts those truths necessary for life that are suprarational but it also imparts *all* truths necessary for life that are not self-evident and thus known to every man without further ado. Thus, for example, and above all, Revelation teaches the existence, unity, and incorporeality of God just as it teaches the createdness of the world. This is necessary, because the truths that are necessary for life, though in principle accessible to reason, are not self-evident and only become accessible to reason after strenuous, long-lasting preparation, although every man needs these truths at all times.[74] Thus, Revelation (at least, its literal meaning) directs itself to all men and not especially to philosophers, and, on the other hand, the man suited to philosophizing, and only he, is authorized and even obligated by Revelation to know the world of man that is accessible in principle to human reason. Therefore the philosopher, who is privileged by his special obligation, neither needs nor can allow himself to be led and bound in the execution of his strictly limited task by (the literal meaning of) Revelation. For Revelation (at least in its literal meaning) wishes to tell the philosopher nothing about things whose knowledge he can reach by himself and whose knowledge is not necessary for life for all men.

Whatever one may think about this arrangement between reason and Revelation suggested by Maimonides, in any case Maimonides unambiguously postulates an essential surplus of the truth of Revelation over the truth of reason. At least on this point there is full concurrence between Maimonides and Judah Halevi,[75] i.e., between the two leading minds of Jewish medieval philosophy. Therefore, Guttmann's assertion that the teaching of the identity of the truth of Revelation with the truth of reason was dominant in Jewish medieval philosophy does not correspond to the facts. The special circumstance that Saadia teaches the identity of the truth of Revelation and the truth of reason (assuming that he really does) can confidently be neglected in a summary judgement of Jewish medieval philosophy, with the same reason and right that Guttmann abstracts from Saadia in his summary comparison of medieval and modern philosophy.[76] For Saadia, who lived before the actual unfolding of Philosophy, *could* not have had as clear a conception of the difficulties of recognizing the teaching of Revelation through reason alone as the men who had to come to terms with Aristotelianism. And as for the later rationalists, we recall Ibn Daud's judgement about the part of the revealed Law that reason cannot penetrate: precisely *because* it is not accessible to reason, it has the advantage that it makes complete obedience to God possible for man. If, however, the realization of this highest virtue—the virtue Abraham displayed in exemplary fashion in the binding of his son—[77] is totally dependent on there being impenetrable commandments of Revelation, then one cannot speak of the sufficiency of reason. And finally we recall Levi Ben Gerson, who "may be the truest disciple of Aristotle that medieval Jewish philosophy produced."[78] To Maimonides' assertion of the insufficiency of reason he even explicitly contraposed the assertion that human reason is sufficient to answer all the questions for whose answers man has a natural desire. Nonetheless, according to his view, the Torah, as the work of infinite wisdom, is accessible to finite reason only in a very limited compass. To be sure, reason and only reason has the key to the Torah, but the Torah is a whole *world*, an analogy to the Creation, enigmatic and full of secrets, and it does not become less so even if its basic teachings, especially the teaching of Creation, can also be known with great difficulty by the independent reason of man.[79]

Now to be sure—we admit it—these conclusions, which so to speak only limit the range of application of Guttmann's conception of "Revelation-believing rationalism," only push back the fundamental question of the inner possibility of a "Revelation-believing rationalism," which as Guttmann depicts it, asserts a complete congruence of the truths of Revelation and reason. As with all fundamental questions, here too *one* case must count for thousands. And Guttmann can name more than one medieval philosopher who asserts the "identity of the truths of Revelation and reason." Indeed, this includes not just philosophers like Saadia, about whom one can raise the objection we have previously mentioned, but rather no less than *the* "Philosophers," i.e., the Islamic Aristotelians from Alfarabi to Averroes. Considering the decisive influence these philosophers exercised precisely in the heyday of Jewish medieval philosophy, and especially on Jewish medieval "philosophy of religion," even if there were no single Jewish philosopher of significance who taught the "identity of the truths of Revelation and reason," we would still have to repeat the question: How is a "Revelation-believing rationalism" of this kind at all understandable?

Such a rationalism was incomprehensible on the basis of Guttmann's depiction because the *interest* the "Revelation-believing rationalists" had in Revelation did not emerge from it. Thus we turn to these philosophers themselves, asking what in their opinion actually is the meaning and purpose of Revelation. In this, we follow Guttmann's reminder that

> In fact one must always remain conscious that a transposition of thoughts is signified if we place the medieval teachings of the purpose and goal of *Revelation* into the perspective of the concept of *religion*, and it does not lose this character even if the purpose of Revelation is identified with that of reason.[80]

Since an essential modification of the state of historical fact is given just with the use of the concept of "religion" and with the assumption that the medieval philosophers taught a "philosophy of religion," we ask first of all: According to the opinion of these philosophers, what is the philosophic discipline whose subject is enlightenment about the meaning and purpose of Revelation?

V

Revelation, as the Law given by God through a prophet, becomes a theme of philosophy in the teaching of prophecy.[81] Of course, psychology treats the natural conditions of the possibility of prophecy, the powers of soul whose highest intensification is the prophetic faculties. But psychology does not deal with prophecy as such, as proved already by the fact that this science deals only incidentally, not comprehensively, with the prophetic faculties. Above all, psychology gives no information about the meaning and purpose of prophecy. This characteristic problem of prophecy is the object of *politics*. Since, however, politics stands in the last place in the structure of the sciences, the question of what place the philosophical grounding of the Law has in the structure of teachings of medieval philosophy is thereby answered. It does not stand at the beginning nor at the midpoint, but rather it is the end and the conclusion, the crowning and seal, if one will, of metaphysics.

But politics proceeds in the following way. It starts from man's being by nature a political life form, and it shows that the human race needs laws and therefore a lawgiver. Now there are two kinds of laws and thus of lawgivers. First, there are laws that have no further task than that of making possible a peaceful living together, which *thus* look only to the health of the body. Second, there are laws that have as their purpose not only the health of the body but also at the same time the health and perfection of the soul. Laws of the first kind are human laws. By contrast, a law that has as its goal the perfection of the soul, or more precisely, the perfection of the intellect, which strives as well for the well-being of the body only for the sake of and toward this characteristically human perfection, is a *divine* law and its proclaimer can only be a *prophet*. But the prophet could not give correct instructions for perfecting the intellect; in other words, he could not call up and educate suitable men to philosophizing if he were not himself a philosopher. The prophet must thus *also* be a philosopher. And indeed, he must be in full possession of philosophical insight if the law that he gives is able to obligate all philosophers. But he may not *only* be a philosopher, for a philosopher, as such, is not suited to be a lawgiver. This is because the art of lawgiving presupposes a perfection of the power of *imagination*, which is not only not characteristic of and hence not necessary for the philosopher but is even a hindrance for him. The prophet is thus teacher and leader, philosopher and lawgiver *in one*. And since he could not be a leader without the faculty of knowledge of the future and of performing miracles, he is philosopher-lawgiver-seer-miracle worker in one.

Now it becomes clear why the philosopher, even in the case that he can know by himself all the truth communicated by the prophets, still is *dependent* upon Revelation and still has an *interest* in Revelation. The philosopher is dependent on Revelation as truly as he is a *man*, for as a man he is a political being and thus in need of a law. And as a rational man, everything must be at stake for him in living under a rational law, i.e., one that is directed to the proper perfection of man. But the philosopher can neither give this to himself nor to others. For as a philosopher, he can indeed *know* the principles of law as such and especially the principles of rational law, but he can never *divine* the concrete individual decrees of the ideal law, through whose precise decrees the Law first becomes applicable and, even more, first becomes law as such. The philosopher thus has an interest in Revelation because he is essentially a man and because man is essentially a political being.

It would be presumptuous to have the pretention to teach an expert like Guttmann about facts that are of course known to him.[82] We dare only dispute with him about their significance, which, in our view, he underestimates in that he does not treat these facts as central. It is not coincidental that he proceeds in this way, but rather is the necessary consequence of his presupposition. Convinced, not of *the* but of a *certain* superiority of modern over medieval philosophy, he does not see himself compelled to a radical critique of the basic modern concepts and formulations of the question. Thus it happens that he who, appropriately, recognizes the Jewish tradition as the judge over modern thought has no misgivings about entrusting the understanding preservation of this tradition to the "philosophy of religion," as the analysis of religious consciousness. As a result, the problem of religious truth, like the problem of the relationship of the theoretical to the religious consciousness of truth, becomes for him the central problem of the "philosophy of religion," and he therefore exerts himself to pursue the germination of this formulation of the question in medieval philosophy. Thus his depiction creates the appearance that for the rationalists of the Middle Ages the *primary* purpose of Revelation was the communication of *truths*, not the proclamation of the *Law*. And since according to the view of these rationalists, the truths communicated through Revelation are also accessible to unassisted reason, there arises the even more problematic appearance that these philosophers ultimately and in earnest only granted Revelation a merely popular pedagogic significance. With Guttmann, the society-founding, *state-founding* meaning of Revelation becomes a subsidiary purpose.[83] Since, then, this mistaking of the leading thought of medieval philosophy is the consequence of Guttmann's modern formulation of the question, and since holding firm to this formulation is the consequence of the conviction that there is a certain superiority of modern over medieval philosophy, we would like to opine that the historian of medieval philosophy would do well to assume, at least heuristically, the *unconditional* superiority of medieval over modern philosophy.

The idea of the "philosophy of religion" that guides Guttmann's research goes back to Schleiermacher. Only with Schleiermacher did it become possible to gain a concept of "religion," a "concept of faith" that is more suited to the "inwardness of the religious consciousness" than the "concept of faith" of the Middle Ages, which, whether rationalist or supernaturalist, was in any case "intellectualist."[84] The return or retreat to "inwardness" has as a consequence or a presupposition the devaluation of all that cannot proceed essentially out of "inwardness." In "inwardness," in "moral consciousness," however, there are founded at most "the general ethical norms," "the unwritten laws,"[85] the principles of human living together and *natural right*, but not the individual determinations by which these principles first become *applicable*. Guttmann therefore remains true to himself when he characterizes these individual decrees which, according to the teaching of Saadia and "many later Jewish thinkers," could only be laid down by Revelation in a suitable way, as "norms of right of a purely technical kind"; when he reproaches Saadia and his successors because they do not distinguish these "norms of right of a purely technical kind . . . from the ethical commandments themselves"[86]; and when he generally qualifies as "primitive" the argument adduced by the aforementioned philosophers that "the most general ethical norms" need "supplementing by means of Revelation."[87]

We would accept this qualification, if only in its primitive, original meaning. The Islamic and Jewish philosophers of the Middle Ages are "more primitive" than the modern philosophers because they are not, like the latter, guided by the derived idea of natural right but rather by the *original, ancient* idea of the *Law* as a unitary, total order of human life—in other words, because they are the disciples of Plato and not the disciples of Christians.[88]

According to the teaching of the Islamic Aristotelians, which was transplanted by Maimonides in particular into Judaism, the prophet, as philosopher and lawgiver in one, is the promulgator of a Law that looks to the perfection characteristic of man. Every law, however, aims to make living together possible. Therefore the prophet is the founder of a society that is directed to the proper perfection of man; he is thus the founder of the ideal state. The classic model of the ideal state is the *Platonic* state. In fact, and even explicitly and programmatically, the Islamic Aristotelians understand the ideal state founded by the prophet according to the Platonic injunction. They understand the prophet as the founder of the Platonic state, as a Platonic philosopher-king. The prophetic lawgiver has fulfilled what the philosopher Plato had demanded, had only been able to demand. Through Plato's demand that philosophy and the direction of the state must coincide, through Plato's idea of the philosopher-king, the framework was established which, taking into account the completed fulfillment of actual Revelation, yields the concept of the prophet of the Islamic Aristotelians and their Jewish disciples.

If this is the case, however, then medieval prophetology (i.e., the medieval philosophical grounding of the Law and hence the medieval "philosophy of religion") is so little *the* original achievement of medieval thought that it is rather nothing other than a modification, or, if one will, the completion of a teaching descended from antiquity. The progression from the philosopher-king to the prophet as philosopher-lawgiver is under no circumstances a more independent achievement than the progression from the Demiurge of the Platonic *Timaeus* to the Creator-God of Revelation. Now it is admittedly correct that, to say the least, the transformation of Platonic (respectively Aristotelian) metaphysics by the Islamic Aristotelians according to the meaning of Revelation's teaching of the Creation was not completed with the same sureness and unambiguousness as the transformation of Platonic politics into a philosophical grounding of the revealed Law. That is why precisely the "most radical" medieval rationalists, who in metaphysics give up all or almost all the teachings that are characteristic of revelation for the Greek philosophical teachings, nonetheless are *relatively* the most original in the realm of the "philosophy of religion." Namely, insofar as they give, in any case, a new answer in their philosophical grounding of the Law—admittedly, a new answer to the old, ancient question about the ideal state and its possibility.

As has been shown, however, external appearances notwithstanding, the philosophical grounding of the Law is not *one* teaching among others but rather the place in the structure of teachings of the Islamic Aristotelians and their Jewish disciples where the presupposition of their philosophizing comes under discussion. If, then, they follow Plato in the philosophical grounding of the Law, one says thereby that these philosophers are Platonists. It is not because they accept this or that Platonic theorem (in this sense they are much more Aristotelian than Platonists) but rather because they are led by Plato in the foundation of philosophizing itself, because they answer a Platonic question in a framework staked out by Plato. In the end, they distinguish themselves from Plato only and to be sure through this. For them, the founder of the ideal state is not a possible philosopher-king who is to be awaited in the future, but rather a real prophet who actually existed in the past. This means that they modify Plato's answer to take account of a Revelation that has now become real. It is from here that the question we characterized above as the central difficulty for the interpretation of Islamic and Jewish medieval rationalism must be answered: Why is the philosophical grounding of the Law, which, it follows, is the philosophical discussion of the presupposition of philosophizing itself, still only one theme among others for these medieval philosophers, and indeed the last theme of their philosophy? The reason for this peculiar disproportion is that they do not have to *look for* the ideal law, as Plato does, because it is *given* by Revelation. Rather, it only needs to be *understood* on the grounds of the principles of the preceding disciplines (metaphysics and psychology). Thus, because for them the Law is not actually *questionable*, not *worth* questioning, their philosophy of the Law does not have the sharpness, originality,[89] depth, and ambiguity of Platonic politics. Because Plato's demand has now been *fulfilled*, Plato's questionings about that demand are therefore *dismissed*.

Through the knowledge of the *essential* dependence of the Islamic Aristotelians and their Jewish disciples on Plato, the concrete possibility of a coherent and original interpretation of the teaching of these medieval philosophers is sketched out. This teaching must be understood as *fundamentally* derived from Platonic philosophy. It is not sufficient to trace it back to Platonic philosophy, verifying it by exact source analysis. On the contrary, the *emergence* of this teaching out of Platonic philosophy must be grasped in its possibility. For this purpose, one must first establish the highest point of perspective whose mutual recognition unites Plato and the medieval thinkers. This point of perspective proves to be the idea of a rational law, i.e., one directed toward the characteristic perfection of man. Such a law—and only such a law deserves the name of "Law"—can, however, only be of divine descent.[90] The idea of the *divine Law* is that sought, highest point of perspective. That is why the interpretation of Platonic philosophy, which is the indispensable presupposition for a radical interpretation of Islamic and Jewish medieval philosophy, must begin not with the *Republic* but with the *Laws*. It is in the *Laws* that Plato undoubtedly stands closest to the world of the revealed

Law, where, by means of a mode of explication that anticipates the philosophical explication of the revealed Law in the medieval thinkers, he transforms the "divine laws" of Greek antiquity into truly divine law; that is, he recognizes them again as truly divine laws. In this drawing nigh to Revelation, (a drawing nigh unguided by Revelation), we grasp at its origins the unbelieving, philosophical foundation of the belief in Revelation. Plato's approach to Revelation offers the medieval thinkers the *starting point* from which they can understand it philosophically. But if Plato was not to lead them astray from Revelation, Platonic philosophy would have to suffer in principle from an *aporia* that was only transcended by Revelation. The radical interpretation of the Islamic Aristotelians and their Jewish disciples thus presupposes an interpretation of the Platonic *Laws* that takes into account that the *Laws point*, but *only* point, to Revelation.

The next step is the investigation of the modifications Platonic politics undergo in the Hellenistic era; in this epoch the transformation of the concept of the philosopher-king into the concept of the prophet is completed. Only when the prophetology of the Islamic Aristotelians (which, it appears, even before Alfarabi has a history that is not exactly short) is understood accordingly can Maimonides' prophetology, which is the most developed form of medieval prophetology as such, be interpreted. In respect to the latter, special clarification is needed as to why the political adjustment, glimmering through everywhere, does not become explicit in Maimonides' prophetology as it does in that of the Islamic Aristotelians. The reason for this fact probably is that for Maimonides, in contrast to his Islamic teachers, Revelation also has the function of communicating teachings that reason cannot sufficiently attest to. Therefore the prophetology of Rabbi Levi ben Gerson commands special interest. It is the actual crux of interpretation. For Levi neither recognizes truths that are suprarational in principle, to which only Revelation could attest, nor ascribes an essentially political meaning to prophecy. According to his teaching, the function of prophecy is primarily divination. Thus it is in Levi that we first find a "Revelation-believing rationalism" that, without having an interest in Revelation, still believes in it and makes it, like all other facts, into an object of philosophical investigation. It is precisely with Levi that we can see how this "Revelation-believing rationalism" only became possible through the disintegration of Platonism. Levi explicitly explains that human care for the continuity of human associations, which Plato held to be necessary, is fundamentally dispensable because this continuity is sufficiently guranteed by Providence. The Platonic ideal state does not first have to be produced by men, not even by prophets—the world and the world of men ruled by Providence are already the ideal state.[91] Providence, which, according to the teaching of the Islamic Aristotelians and Maimonides, is the condition for the necessary fulfillment of the desideratum of a prophetic lawgiving and state-founding, according to Levi's assertion, does not even let it come to this desideratum. According to Plato, the question of the law, at first the necessity of human care for human beings, has its ground in the absence of divine caring,[92] and accordingly, the realization of the ideal state depends on chance.[93] For Levi's medieval predecessors—following the belief in Revelation that is grounded on the belief in Providence—the ideal state "only" loses its questionableness. But the ideal state loses its meaning as such through Levi's completed "radicalization" of the idea of Providence.

Levi thus does not merely approach "modern deism";[94] at once, and in an astonishing way, he approaches that kind of modern politics that first explicitly and then implicitly believes it can encompass the activity of the state in the very narrowest limits. It believes this on the grounds of an apparently radicalized, but in truth abstract, belief in Providence that overlooks the power of evil. From this point, finally, Mendelssohn's teaching of Revelation, which despite the "radicalization" of the belief in Providence and despite even the surrender of the traditional natural right of obligation in favor of the modern natural right of claims[95] seeks to restore the Platonic-medieval thoughts of law, can be illuminated in all its questionableness.

The necessary connection between politics and theology (metaphysics), which we stumbled on by chance, guarantees that the interpretation of the Jewish philosophy of the Middle

Ages that begins in Platonic politics (and not with the *Timaeus* or Aristotle's *Metaphysics*) cannot lose sight of the metaphysical problems that stand in the foreground for the medieval philosophers themselves. This procedure, far from leading to an underestimation of these problems, much rather offers the single assurance for the understanding of its characteristic, i.e., its human meaning. If, by contrast, as the history of previous scholarship plainly shows, one proceeds from the metaphysical problems, then one misses the political problem, in which nothing less than the foundation of philosophy is hidden, the philosophical enlightenment of the presupposition of philosophizing.

It is Guttmann's great merit to have pointed to the deeper presuppositions of medieval metaphysics by bringing out the "religious-philosophical" character of medieval philosophy. On the basis of the critical analysis of the *modern* concept of "religious consciousness" and of a renewed understanding of the *ancient*, Platonic concept of the divine law, it will have to be the task of future scholarship to help Guttmann's actual intention, which betrays itself most clearly in the fact of his energetic preoccupation with medieval philosophy, to achieve victory. In this way, too, the deep intuition of Hermann Cohen will finally receive its due: that Maimonides was "in deeper harmony with Plato than with Aristotle."[96]

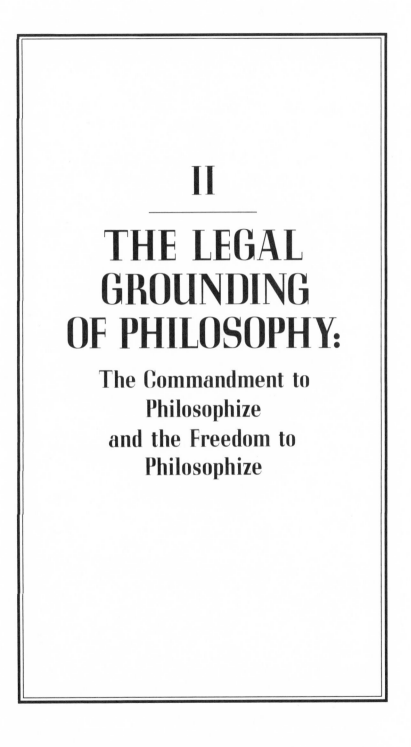

II

THE LEGAL GROUNDING OF PHILOSOPHY:

The Commandment to
Philosophize
and the Freedom to
Philosophize

The men from whose teaching the philosophical and hence unbelieving foundation of medieval Jewish (and Islamic) philosophy is most approachable, i.e., the medieval rationalists, have more or less extensively and comprehensively developed a legal grounding of philosophy, i.e., a justification of philosophizing before the forum of Revelation. Even in the case that this or that rationalist did not intend honestly the legal grounding of philosophy and wrote it only to soothe others' suspicions, this fact is already sufficient proof that the reality of Revelation, of the revealed Law, is the decisive prephilosophical presupposition of these philosophers. Though once they have assured themselves of the permission or the commandment to philosophize as such, they may clarify[1] philosophically the possibility of Revelation and may even finally look upon reason as the only judge of the truth or falsity of Revelation. Thus the fact of revelation is secured *before* all efforts and convictions of that kind, before *all* philosophizing. It makes no difference in this respect whether this fact is recognized on the ground of an immediate insight into the superhuman descent of the source of Revelation or on the ground of a mediated, historical proof. For both the immediate insight as well as the proof are independent of all specific philosophical deliberation, especially of reflection about the conditions of possibility of Revelation in general, and they accordingly precede the legal grounding of philosophy and thereby philosophizing itself.

Thus, under the prephilosophical presupposition of the fact of Revelation and *only*, though necessarily, under that presupposition, one comes to the desideratum of a legal grounding of philosophy. For the revealed Law, for the time being, makes philosophizing questionable through and through. A law given by God and thus perfect is necessarily sufficient to guide life to its true goal. But what meaning, then, does philosophizing have? Does it not necessarily lose its seriousness? Or, if it keeps its seriousness, does it not then necessarily lead away from the *one* duty and task of man, of the Jew? What has the Jew to do with Plato and Aristotle that he should keep watch at their door to learn wisdom from them? Are not the works of these philosophers profane books that seduce the heart with fictitious opinions and erroneous views?[2] Stated fundamentally: Is philosophizing forbidden, permitted, or even commanded?

In the following we will see how Averroes, Maimonides, and Rabbi Levi ben Gerson answer this question. We begin with Averroes because he propounds the legal grounding of philosophy comprehensively in a treatise devoted specifically to this purpose, the *Facl-ul-maqāl*.[3] Our primary interest is in Maimonides, the "classic of rationalism" in Judaism. In order to understand better Maimonides' "moderate" rationalism, one must look ahead to the far more "radical" view that Rabbi ben Gerson develops in an explicit polemic against Maimonides. In Levi's "radical" teaching, one can recognize more sharply than in Maimonides' "moderate" teaching what "rationalism" in medieval Judaism is all about.

AVERROES

The purpose of the *Facl-ul-maqāl* is the "determination of the connection that exists between the Law and philosophy." The investigation expressly has the character of *legal* speculation.[4] It asks whether speculation about philosophy and the sciences of logic is *permitted, forbidden, or ordered* by the Law.[5] In the form Averroes uses, the distinction among these qualifications is taken from the (Islamic) Law itself. It is of fundamental importance in this Law; it and the question made precise by it find fundamental application in all human dealings.[6] For the time being, philosophy thus has no priority whatsoever over any other human activity. Like every other human activity, it stands under the Law and must answer to the Law.

By philosophy is understood the contemplation of existing things in reference to their Artisan.[7] So understood, philosophy, whose organ is reason, is, however, made into a *duty* by the Law, as countless verses of the Koran undoubtedly attest.[8] From this derives the *duty* to occupy oneself with logic, whose objects—the kinds and conditions of rational conclusions—relate to speculation as tools to labor.[9] In case predecessors have already worked on logic, there emerges from this their successors' *duty* to seek help from their predecessors, whether coreligionists or not, "for, as long as the instrument that serves for slaughter contains in itself the conditions of validity, in terms of the validity of the completed slaughter, one does not pay attention to whether it belongs to one of our coreligionists or to one who is not a coreligionist."[10] Herewith, pursuit of Aristotelian logic is derived as a *duty* imposed by the Law. It is established in the same way that it is a legal *duty* to study the philosophical books of one's predecessors, that is, those books that have as their object existing things in their reference to their Artisan.[11] Thus the study of Aristotle's physics and metaphysics is also a *duty*.

Philosophy stands *under the Law*, but in such a way that it is *commanded* by the Law. And indeed, it is not even commanded as one among many human activities; rather its characteristic purpose is identical with the purpose of the Law. Distinctively, the grounding of this much more extensive assertion does not emerge plainly in Averroes' exposition; he has above all to deal with a legal, i.e., casuistic consideration. The grounding of the more extensive assertion, which becomes noticeable at various places in the casuistic consideration, goes like this. The *purpose of the Law* is to summon men to bliss. Bliss consists of the *knowledge of God.* Now one can only know God from existing things, for these, as produced by God, point to God as their Producer. The consideration of existing things as pointing to their Producer—that and nothing else is philosophizing. Thus the purpose of philosophy is identical to the purpose of Law. It would therefore be the highest degree of folly and of separation from God—and not just one punishable act among many—to prevent one who is suited to philosophize from philosophizing.[12]

The Legal Grounding of Philosophy

It does not matter now if the commandment to philosophize is *one* commandment among many or *the* commandment. "For, since these (namely the religious) laws are truth and summon to speculation, which leads to the knowledge of truth, so we Muslims know positively that the speculation that proceeds by means of demonstration does not lead to the opposite of what is revealed by the Law. For truth does not conflict with truth, but is in accord with and witnesses truth."[13] Philosophy and law cannot conflict with each other because they are both truth, because both go back to the source of truth, to God, the giver of the Law and the Creator of reason. One must now note, however, that while this deliberation excludes *a priori* any conflict between philosophy and Law, it does not provide a basis for the *right* to philosophize. The right to philosophize bases itself solely on the explicit commandment of the Law ("since these laws . . . summon to consideration"). The creation of reason is one thing; its institution and authorization are another.

Reason, which is authorized to philosophize by the Law, philosophy, which is commanded by the Law, just because of that cannot come into conflict with the Law. If now philosophy leads to some kind of knowledge of some thing, and the Law speaks of this thing differently than philosophy, then the maxim of the Law needs *interpretation.* That is, this maxim may not be understood literally, but rather figuratively.[14] It *must* be understood figuratively; interpretation also is *duty,* although only for the "people of demonstration," for the men suited to philosophizing. For the rest it is *forbidden.* Therefore the people of demonstration are *commanded* to keep the interpretation secret from other men. Whoever, whether philosopher or non-philosopher, trespasses against this commandment or prohibition makes himself guilty of *unbelief* (denial) or at least of *heresy* (innovation).[15] Thus those who are suited to philosophize are commanded (1) to philosophize, (2) to interpret the Law, in case of a conflict between philosophy and the literal meaning of the Law, and (3) to keep the interpretation secret from all the unchosen.

Is the philosophy authorized by the Law *free?* Can philosophy teach everything that it itself establishes, *unencumbered by the Law*? Is it *not in need* of guidance by the Law? The freedom of the philosophy that is authorized by the Law, with respect to the Law, is guaranteed by the right of interpretation: Is this right without any limit whatsoever? Averroes establishes five limitations, which we wish to examine in the order of their scope.

1. Interpretation may not be contrary to Arabic linguistic usage; it must follow the rules of art.[16] The freedom to philosophize is not impaired by this limitation. To see this, one has only to reflect that a maxim of the Law that contradicts reason and that may not be interpreted according to the rules of art can at any time be conceived as intended merely rhetorically, as merely valid for the many. The interpretation of the Law as a whole makes the "interpretation" of the individual texts dispensable in some circumstances. How little the stated condition limits interpretation is shown, for example, by the interpretation of the Koran verse: "Summon to the way of your Lord by wisdom and by the beautiful admonition, and struggle with them through that which is most beautiful." This verse is said to refer plainly to three methods of convincing: "wisdom" to demonstrative argumentation, "beautiful admonition" to rhetoric, and "struggling" to dialectic.[17]

2. If the literal meaning of the Law contradicts the result of demonstrations and thus must be interpreted, after thorough study of the Law, one will always find a passage whose literal meaning "confirms this interpretation or comes close to confirming it."[18] If one reflects that there is probably scarcely a philosophical doctrine of which it cannot be said that there are passages in Scripture that "confirm or come close to confirming it," one sees that this second limitation is also not really a limitation.

3. Passages that, according to the true consensus of Muslims, are to be understood literally, may not be interpreted. On this, Averroes himself says that a true consensus can never be established in speculative things, if only because, according to a view widespread in the beginning period of Islam, the "inner" meaning, which varies from the literal meaning, may not be publicly communicated.[19]

The Legal Grounding of Philosophy

4. Teachings known by all three kinds of convincing—demonstrative, dialectical, and rhetorical argumentation—may not be interpreted.[20] This does not even formally involve a limitation of the right of interpretation. For, since the possibility and necessity of interpreting a passsage in the Law only exist if this passage conflicts with the result of demonstration, then it is clear that there is no call to interpret a passage whose literal meaning is *also* confirmed by demonstration.[21]

5. Interpretation may not lead to denial of the *existence* of things that belong to the principles of the Law. Interpretation is only possible in regard to the *quality* of these things. (For example, the existence of future life may not be denied, though one may have a different opinion about its quality than the Koran's literal meaning.[22]) These principles are also and precisely accessible, however, to philosophical knowledge.[23] Thus there is no reason for the philosopher to interpret the passages in the Koran that deal with them.

Therefore, in every case of a contradiction between philosophy and Law, the philosopher may interpret the literal meaning of the Law and is not bound by it. In that sense, philosophy is *free*. This freedom would, however, become doubtful if "the error, which encounters the learned when they speculate about the difficult things that the Law has commissioned them to speculate about," were a sin. So Averroes also asserts that errors of this kind are excusable, and that not only the one suited for philosophy who knows the truth earns God's reward but also the one suited to philosophy who errs in the course of his philosophizing.[24] To be sure, he only goes that far in connection with the discussion of a question whose answer he holds to be dogmatically irrelevant.[25] Fundamentally, he teaches: "In general, error in relation to the Law is twofold. Either it is an error for which he is excused who is worthy of speculating about that wherein the error occurred . . . or it is an error for which no man is excused, which is *denial* if it occurs in the principles of the Law, and *innovation* if it occurs in the derived teachings."[26] In this sense, then, philosophy is *bound*.

One can, at first, doubt whether this bondage is distinguished from the bondage given by the intention of philosophy itself, bondage to known truth. For since the "principles of the

Law" deal with truths accessible to philosophy itself, philosophy itself qualifies deviation from these principles as error. Yet philosophy does not supply the decisive qualification of error in relation to these principles (decisive because it decides on the excusableness or inexcusableness of error), the qualification of error as "denial" (unbelief). This qualification stems from the Law. In binding philosophy, it binds it through an extraphilosophical, prephilosophical jurisdiction. Put differently, there are *dogmas* for Averroes, though they are accessible to independent human reason and hence are not "dogmas" in the sense of supernatural truths. However, the acknowledgment or denial of these truths of reason has entirely the character and consequences of acknowledgment or denial of a dogma. If the word "dogmas" gives offense, one must at least say that for Averroes there are *truths prescribed by the Law.*

The philosophy authorized by the Law thus is not free in the sense that one could simply not say in advance what it will teach. It is not as if it goes its way, wholly unguided, finding out in surprise at the end that what has resulted is also and already given by the Law; rather, its results are already known in advance, just through the Law, and error in relation to these results is announced in advance as inexcusable. This bondage of philosophy already expresses itself in its definition: it is nothing other than the knowledge of God from the perspective of Creation. In the end, philosophy does nothing more than to deepen and prove the knowledge that is accessible to *all* Muslims through the Law.[27]

Philosophy owes its authorization, its freedom, to the Law; *its freedom rests on its bondage.* Philosophy is not sovereign. The beginning of philosophy is not the beginning simply. The Law has primacy. The literal meaning of the Law may only be surrendered when the contrary is *proved;* it is not that one assumes *in advance* a standpoint outside the Law, from which one progresses, on the path of rational deliberation, to subjection under the Law. Under these circumstances, the possibility exists that the Law teaches all sorts of things that are not accessible to philosophy and that *therefore* cannot and may not be interpreted. In fact, in two of Averroes' texts (the *Tahāfut al-tahāfut* and the *Manāhij*), there are a number of passages in which he speaks of the content of Revelation as exceeding rational knowledge, and of the *superiority* of Revelation over reason.[28] There is controversy about whether one can wholly trust such utterances. In any case, it would be worthwhile to point them out emphatically as long as it were still important to make clear that Averroes was not, say, the Voltaire of the twelfth century. But even for this proof, these utterances would not be indispensable, for proof is already furnished by Averroes' unambiguous acknowledgment of the primacy of the Law. But if this primacy is secure, then the question of whether philosophy, authorized by the Law, is by its own strength wholly or partially able to know the truths taught by the Law (and therewith the controversy about Averroes' aforementioned "believing" utterances) becomes in any case of only secondary significance.[29]

MAIMONIDES

Since the legal grounding of philosophy is not the theme of the *Guide of the Perplexed*, one will not find in this book as connected an explication as we find in Averroes' *Facl-ul-maqāl*. One must therefore put together Maimonides' relevant utterances from the different parts of his work.[30]

The Law calls for belief in the most important truths (God's existence, unity, and so forth). Belief is, however, not just confession with the lips, but rather understanding of what is believed. Belief is only then perfect when a man has seen that the opposite of what is believed is in no way possible. The Law thus calls for understanding and for the proof of the truths it communicates. It thereby implicitly commands knowledge of the world, for God is only knowable from His works. To be sure, the Law has not expressly communicated this knowledge, but, in commanding that God should be loved and feared, it commands knowledge of the world as the way to the love and fear of God. The appropriation of the truths prescribed by the Law presupposes many prior studies—mathematics, logic and physics.[31]

Scripture and tradition prove that as God's activity is perfect as such, so too is the Law given by Him. This Law—the Law as a whole and every single commandment—necessarily has a basis, a rational purpose. Divine Law distinguishes itself from human laws in that it serves the highest purpose, the proper perfection of man. The proper perfection of man is knowledge, the knowledge of God.[32] The purpose of the Law is thus identical to the purpose of philosophy.

If philosophy, authorized by the Law, leads to a result that conflicts with the literal meaning of the Law, and *thus* the literal meaning is impossible, then we must interpret the literal meaning, i.e., consider it as meant figuratively.[33] All the passages of Scripture that assign corporeality and mutability to God must especially be interpreted. In this case, it is even a duty to communicate to the many that the relevant passages may not be understood literally; no man may be left with the belief of the corporeality of God, just as he may not be left with the belief in the nonexistence of God or the existence of many gods.[34] But one may only communicate the elements of the other subjects of metaphysics, of the "secrets of the Torah," and that only to suitable persons. The many must be hindered from occupying themselves with these subjects; it is *legally prohibited* to teach them publicly.[35]

Maimonides thus agrees with Averroes that the Law commands (1) philosophizing, (2) interpreting the literal meaning in case of a contradiction between philosophy and the literal meaning of the Law, and (3) keeping secret the interpretation from all those not called to it.[36] Therefore one must ask Maimonides, as before we asked Averroes: Is the right of interpretation without any limits? The question has been made much more pointed. Is Revelation (the Law) superior to reason in that it conveys truths that reason cannot contradict because they are not accessible to it? Maimonides' answer is beyond doubt: Human intellect has a limit beyond which it cannot go. Therefore, for the honor of his Lord, man is obligated to stop at this limit and not to reject the teachings of Revelation that he cannot intuit and prove.[37] Philosophy is free in its realm. Its realm is nature, not the supernatural. To be more exact, its realm is the world beneath the heavens, not the heavens; its realm is the world of man.[38]

Maimonides speaks about the inferiority of human intellect with regard to Revelation, above all in connection with his discussions of the problem of Creation. He decides that it is impossible for men to answer the question, "Is the world eternal or created?" by scientific means. Science can indeed weaken the arguments of the "philosophers" for the eternity of the world; even further, it can make probable the creation of the world. But science cannot prove it; it must finally leave the question unanswered and accept the solution offered by Revelation.[39] With this, Maimonides acknowledges a supernatural truth as such.

From here, we glance back to Averroes' teaching. We left open the question of whether Averroes acknowledged supernatural truths or not. Against an affirmative answer, it has been proposed that, if only because Islam does not know a spiritual office of teaching, there could not be supernatural truths for Averroes.[40] We now see that in any case this argument has no probative power, because Judaism also has no spiritual office of teaching, and yet there is a supernatural truth for Maimondes. Yet while the comparison with Maimonides' teaching annihilates this argument, it also confirms the conception this argument was supposed to serve. Maimonides' assertion of the insufficiency of human intellect gains its concrete meaning as the assertion of the insufficiency of human intellect to answer the question: Which alternative is true, creation of the world or eternity of the world? Then too, Maimonides is certain that Scripture teaches the creation of the world and, what is more important for him, that Judaism loses its basis if the assertion of Creation is surrendered.[41] By contrast, Averroes holds the question of "creation or eternity of the world" to be dogmatically irrelevant.[42] The most important reason that prompted Maimonides to assert the insufficiency of human intellect and its dependence on Revelation therefore disappears. We thus assume that Averroes fundamentally acknowledges the sufficiency of human intellect, and thus that the passages in which he speaks of an excess of the theoretical teachings of Revelation over those of reason need "interpretation."

The question of whether human intellect is sufficient or insufficient, whether or not it needs guidance from Revelation, whether in this sense it is free or bound, proves to be secondary if one considers that the primacy of the Law stands firm for Averroes no less than for Maimonides. Philosophizing is commanded by the Law; philosophy is authorized by the Law. The freedom of philosophy rests on its bondage. According to this presupposition, philosophy, authorized by the Law, is nothing but the understanding (or else the proof) of the truth already communicated by the Law; it is nothing other than the *acquisition of the Law.*

RABBI LEVI BEN GERSON

The philosophical teachings of Levi can be characterized by and large, if by no means in regard to all important points, as a unification of the teachings of Maimonides with those of Averroes. In any case, his teaching of the sufficiency of reason, which will be discussed further on, stands between Maimonides' assertion of the insufficiency and Averroes' assertion of the sufficiency of reason. In that Levi's thought moves between the fixed limits of the positions of Maimonides and Averroes, the primacy of the Law and the meaning of philosophy determined by it are self-evident presuppositions for him.

Like Maimonides in the *Guide of the Perplexed*, in the *Milhamot ha-shem* Levi turns only to those Jews who "have fallen into confusion through these huge questions," and whose intellect does not rest at what one only can express but only at what one understands.[43] He does not first need to prove that philosophy is emancipated by the Law. For that, he can call on Maimonides as his authority. Maimonides has shown that we have to believe what is shown by speculation and that, in the case of a conflict between speculation and the literal meaning of Scripture, the literal meaning is to be interpreted so that it agrees with speculation.[44]

From this, Levi draws a consequence with which—at least, with whose explicit establishment—he goes beyond Maimonides. He takes as his principle *first* to carry through completely the investigation as a scientific investigation and only *then* to make clear that the result of the scientific investigation is the view of the Torah.[45] He thereby grants science a much greater freedom than does Maimonides. He is aware that he thereby deviates from Maimonides. He sees himself as explicitly required to take issue with Maimonides. This taking of issue is the most important subject of the Preface to the *Milḥamot*.

In this Preface, Levi, with the intention of clearing away the objections that could make his enterprise questionable from the outset, first takes issue with the decision Maimonides arrived at in regard to the possibility of mastering scientifically the problem of the creation of the world.[46] He revolts against this decision. It is less astonishing that he is not content with it, since Maimonides himself had made the decision ambiguously, when he had incidentally explained that perhaps someone else possessed a proof for the Creation, that he himself could do no *more* than to confess his embarrassment, and that, in any case, he knew of no proof.[47] Did there not lie in this an invitation to successors to strive for the "knowledge of that which remained concealed to predecessors?"[48] Maimonides' explanation could, however, be conceived quite differently. If even Maimonides, "the crown of the wise," had confessed his inadequacy to solve the problem under discussion, was it not "impudence and presumption"[49] to try one's hand at its solution? Levi counts on this obvious objection. He replies that what had been concealed to the predecessors did not therefore have to remain concealed to the successors, for otherwise no philosopher would know anything he had not learned from others. But, if that is how things were, there would be no science at all. He who deviated from his predecessors did not deserve blame, only he who made erroneous assertions.[50] Levi is determined to take seriously the possibility that Maimonides only hinted at and perhaps did not even mean seriously, namely, that someone other than himself (Maimonides) could master the problem of Creation. Believing that successors can recognize what remained concealed to predecessors and that "time makes possible the ascertainment of truth,"[51] hence believing in the possibility of the progress of science,[52] he doubts Maimonides' decision, which set up an insuperable barrier to science. He stabilizes the right of free investigation, unencumbered by the authority of predecessors, which acknowledges no standard other than factual truth.[53]

Maimonides had spoken of the fact that the philosophers had disputed for three thousand years over the question: Creation of the world or eternity of the world?[54] In another passage, without specific mention of the problem of Creation but certainly not without thinking also and precisely of it, he had stated that there are things for whose knowledge man has "a powerful desire," even though human understanding is not capable of giving a proof of these things. And it is just because man has so strong a desire for knowledge of these things that doubt and conflict arise.[55] Levi also explicitly directs himself to these utterances of Maimonides. He objects that the desire to recognize the truth about the problem of Creation is *natural*. But a natural desire cannot extend to something fundamentally unattainable. Thus the solution of this problem is fundamentally possible, and not, as Maimonides had decided, fundamentally impossible.[56] Whereas for Maimonides the fact that man has this strong desire was rather a ground for warning against the temptation that stems from it,[57] for Levi it is an indication that the desire can be fulfilled. Levi thus does not merely assert the *right* of man to venture to answer questions that his predecessors passed on unanswered or even as unanswerable. Beyond that, he asserts the *adequacy* of man at least to answer the question the present argument directly concerns, the queston: Creation or eternity of the world? But since this question is a central one, and, furthermore the reason Levi gives for the fundamental possibility of answering it correctly establishes beyond doubt the fundamental possibility of answering *all* questions for whose answer man has a natural desire, consequently, Maimonides asserts the insufficiency of human intellect just as generally. Thus, it must be said that Levi sets up the assertion of sufficiency against Maimonides' assertion of insufficiency.

The Legal Grounding of Philosophy

73

Maimonides made it his principle not to set forth the teachings of metaphysics in a clear order and connectedly but rather in various passages in his work and mixed with other subjects. Not just the prohibition expressed in the Law (against publicly communicating the secrets of the Torah) but rather, and above all, factual necessity induced him to abstain from transparency of depiction. The subject of metaphysics is not always and continuously accessible to our sight like the subjects of the other sciences, which can therefore be presented methodically and transparently; rather it shows itself and then quickly withdraws from view. That is why the only proper way of speaking about God is to speak in parables and riddles, and that is why the abstention from parables and riddles necessary for a scientific treatise has the consequence that speech becomes dark and brief.[58] The characteristic manner of communicating metaphysics, esoteric communication, is grounded in man's insufficiency to achieve knowledge of God.

Since Levi replaces the assertion of insufficiency with the assertion of sufficiency, he is relieved of the necessity of using another kind of depiction in metaphysics than that which is usual in the other sciences. He expressly turns against the authors who, by the disposition of their depiction and the darkness of their speech (intending to make their thoughts incomprehensible to the many), make the easy into the difficult. In contrast to these authors, he makes his principle thoroughness of depiction and clarity of disposition.[59] He is not content just to dispute in this way that the public communication of metaphysical teachings is forbidden; he even asserts that this communication is a *duty*. Just as God, out of pure goodness, communicates Being and perfection to all existing things, so man should make others perfect with the perfection he has achieved. And therefore it would be most harmful if man refused to communicate his knowledge to others.[60] Thus, going beyond Maimonides and Averroes, Levi asserts the *freedom of public communication* of philosophical truths—for every communication by books is public communication.[61]

According to what has been said, for Levi, the freedom of philosophizing is to be understood as follows: (1) the right of philosophizing; (2) the complete carrying through of philosophical investigation, wholly unencumbered by the Law; (3) the right to interpret the Law with respect to the truths found by philosophy; and (4) the public communication of the truths found by philosophy. Is philosophy then simply free, according to Levi? We will consider first the *apparent* limitations of philosophical freedom to be found in his writings.

1. Against Maimonides, Levi asserts the sufficiency of philosophy for the mastery of the problem of Creation. Nonetheless, he says in his commentary on the Pentateuch that it is improbable that a philosopher would recognize[62] the truth about Creation by way of speculation if he did not let himself be guided by the Torah.[63] In this sense, he says of his own remarks about Creation that he was guided to them "in a wondrous manner" by the teachings of the Torah.[64] Manifestly he is not taking back the assertion of sufficiency, for the fundamental sufficiency of human intellect to master a problem agrees very well with this mastery's being very difficult and therefore improbable.

2. Levi explains that one must rely on Scripture in regard to the teaching of miracles. How he means this is indicated by the context. Starting with the text has no other character than starting with sense perception. If one wants to investigate a subject fundamentally accessible to sense perception but that is factually not accessible to the investigator in this manner, one must seek help in the reports of others who have at their disposal sense perception of the relevant subject, "just as did the Philosopher in respect to the species of living beings and Ptolemey in respect to the aspects of the stars."[65]

3. In his middle commentary on Aristotle's *Topics*, Averroes had counted among the themes whose dialectical treatment was of use the question of whether the world was created or not. Against this, Levi objects that this subject may not be discussed dialectically but is to be assumed on the grounds of prophecy, which verifies to believers things whose explanation is impossible for unbelieving philosophers. In addition, the dialectical treatment of the problem of Creation does harm, for with the belief in Creation stands or falls belief in the miracles recounted in the Torah, among which is the Torah's Revelation itself.[66] With this, Levi only forbids dialectical treatment

The Legal Grounding of Philosophy

of the problem of Creation, not philosophical treatment as such. Still, it follows from this polemic against Averroes that, unlike him, Levi does not hold the question of Creation to be dogmatically irrelevant, and that he binds himself more closely than Averroes to the teaching of Revelation.

4. Against Averroes, Levi asserts the insufficiency of human intellect to unite with the *intellectus agens*.[67] He objects that, as Averroes himself concedes, the unification presupposes that man has acquired all the concepts the *intellectus agens* has. This presupposition, however, is unfulfillable, for there are, for example, kinds of animals, plants, and minerals of which we can have no concept, because of their smallness or on other grounds.[68] In other passages he speaks of the incapacity of men to know exactly the dependence of the sublunary on the heavenly bodies; the reason for this incapacity is the huge distance, in essence and place, of man from the stars.[69] In the introduction to the commentary on the Pentateuch, he thus summarizes these remarks: it is impossible for us to know fully the wisdom and mercy contained in Creation.

One can begin trying to overcome the discrepancy between this assertion of insufficiency and the assertion of sufficiency set out in the Preface to the *Milḥamot* by having recourse to a passage in the *Guide* undoubtedly considered by Levi. Maimonides divides the subjects for whose knowledge human intellect does not reach into subjects for whose knowledge man has no desire and subjects for whose knowledge man has a great desire. Among the first group are the number of stars and the number of species of animals, minerals, and plants.[70] Now in fact, Levi does speak precisely of the insufficiency of man with respect to his insufficient knowledge of the species of animals, and so forth, and his knowledge of the stars. Further, he asserts the connection between natural desire and sufficiency. One could thus opine that, *against* Maimonides, Levi asserts man's sufficiency to achieve knowledge of all subjects for whose knowledge he has a natural desire, and that, *with* Maimonides, he asserts the insufficiency of man to achieve knowledge of certain subjects for whose knowledge man has no desire.

This solution of the difficulty is, however, impossible. In the same context in which he speaks of insufficiency to achieve knowledge of the stars, Levi asserts that man has a great desire precisely for the knowledge of those "deep subjects." For the more splendid a thing is, the stronger is our desire for knowledge of it, so that we have a stronger desire for a weak knowledge of a splendid thing than for a perfect knowledge of a low thing.[71]

With this, however, Levi seems to contradict himself completely. For, in contradiction to his assertion about the connection between natural desire and sufficiency, he seems to assert that man has the strongest desire precisely for knowledge of those subjects whose knowledge is most difficult. But therein already lies the solution. The knowledge of subjects for which man has the strongest desire is most *difficult* because these subjects are the most sublime and stand farthest from man with respect to essence and place. But—and the naturalness of this desire is an adequate sign—this knowledge is *not impossible*. Therefore, what follows from the difficulty of the investigation is not that "we must keep our hands off this investigation," but, on the contrary, the praiseworthiness and urgency of the investigation.[72] If, then, Levi asserts the insufficiency of man in a certain manner, in any case a limitation of the freedom of research does not follow. For out of insufficiency, as Levi asserts it, it does not follow that a firm barrier to human research can be indicated.

The limitation of philosophical freedom that Levi also acknowledges is in truth much more radical. It does not appear at the end of philosophy but rather lies at its basis.

> It must not remain concealed to us that it is impossible for us to know perfectly what wisdom and mercy are contained in the Being of the Torah; rather, we know little and mistake much of this. Similarly, it is impossible for us to know perfectly what wisdom and mercy are contained in the Being of existing things, as they are; rather, we know little of the wisdom contained in their creation.[73]

Like the world, the Torah is a work of infinite wisdom and mercy and thus is only knowable in small part by finite understanding. The Torah is itself a *world, in* which man lives, for the understanding of which he should exert himself according to his strength, but that always contains *more* wisdom and goodness than man is capable of seeing. The Torah is thus not a barrier to research—since research comes to no barrier in uncovering the wisdom and mercy contained in it—but is a *direction* for research.[74] The Torah is—like the world *as* "world"—*before* philosophy. The primacy of the Law is just as secure for Levi as for Maimonides and Averroes. It remains to ask how these philosophers understand the Law—which in the first instance they have only accepted as real, as given— in terms of its possibility and how they thereby justify it philosophically.

III

THE PHILOSOPHICAL GROUNDING OF THE LAW

Maimonides' Teaching of Prophecy and Its Sources[1]

I

Prophetology is a central teaching of the *Guide of the Perplexed*. One gets an idea of its difficulties[2] from the list of conditions which, according to Maimonides' teaching, the prophet must fulfill. The prophet must have at his command (1) a perfect intellect, (2) perfect morals, (3) a perfect power of imagination, (4) the faculty of daring, (5) the faculty of divination, and (6) the faculty of leadership (of men). What do these different conditions of prophecy have in common? Whence does this rhapsody gain a unitary, transparent order? Orientation must take as its beginning the fact, rightly understood, that prophetology is a central teaching of the *Guide of the Perplexed*. This fact, rightly understood, signifies that the position for whose clarification and defense the *Guide* was written is possible only if there is prophecy in the sense explicated by Maimonides' prophetology. Therefore, understanding this prophetology wholly depends on understanding its assigned position. Starting from a provisional understanding of this position, on its basis we develop that part of the prophetology that can be understood from it in Part I. The other part of Maimonides' prophetology cannot be clarified either in itself or in its connections with the first part from Maimonides' own utterances. The problem is that in his prophetology, Maimonides follows a philosophical tradition that ruled for centuries, whose presuppositions he no longer even mentions. He does not follow this tradition slavishly; on the one hand he restricts its teachings, and on the other he elaborates upon them. But he remains within a compass of questions and possible answers already marked out before him. It therefore becomes necessary to return to his sources; we thus ask about the relationship of his prophetology to the prophetology of Alfarabi and Avicenna. Giving consideration to these sources in Part II, we then interpret the part of his prophetology not discussed

The Philosophical Grounding of the Law

in Part I, and finally, in Part III, we interpret the entire context of his prophetology. The complete interpretation contributes to a deeper understanding of Maimonides' position in Part IV.[3]

II

With a certain right one can characterize Maimonides' position as "religious Enlightenment in the Middle Ages." With a certain right—namely, only if one keeps in mind that freedom of human thought, "freedom of philosophy," mattered to the modern Enlightenment (thus, the *actual* age of Enlightenment, from which one is accustomed to *transfer* the expression "enlightenment" to certain medieval [and also ancient] appearances) as well as to Maimonides and his medieval predecessors and successors.[4] One may not, however, allow an instant's doubt that the medieval philosophers were, in the original understanding, precisely *not* Enlighteners. They were *not* concerned with *spreading* light, with educating the *many* to rational knowledge, with *enlightening*. They constantly impress upon the philosophers the duty *to keep* rationally recognized truth *secret* from the unchosen many. The *esoteric* character of philosophy was unconditionally established for them, in contrast to the actual, i.e., modern, Enlightenment. Certainly there were men, even in the seventeenth and eighteenth centuries who, to cite of all people Voltaire, opined, *"Quand la populace se mêle à raisonner, tout est perdu,"* and, on the other hand, men such as Maimonides cherished a *certain* enlightenment of all.[5] But if one considers that the modern in contrast to the medieval Enlightenment in general *propagates* its teachings, one will not object to the assertion that the medieval Enlightenment was fundamentally esoteric, while the modern Enlightenment was fundamentally exoteric. Even the most provisional characterization of Maimonides' position may not neglect to take into account its specific differentiation from the modern Enlightenment.

The esoteric character of the "religious Enlightenment in the Middle Ages" has its basis in the rule of the ideal of the *theoretical* life, just as the exoteric character of the modern Enlightenment has its basis in the conviction (which ruled long before its Kantian formulation, grounding, and radicalization) of the primacy of *practical* reason. Maimonides' position can therefore be characterized provisionally as follows: it upholds the Greek ideal of the life of *theory*, as classically explicated by Aristotle at the conclusion of the *Nicomachean Ethics*, under the presupposition of *Revelation*. Accordingly, for Maimonides two things are established: first, that Revelation is *simply* binding, and second, for man to be a perfect being, it is *simply* required that he follow the life of theory. These heterogeneous convictions are united in that the summons to and education for the theoretical life are asserted to be the highest (if not also the only) purpose of Revelation. For Scripture commands us "to know God," and the highest subject of theory is the highest being, which is God. Therefore Maimonides teaches that what is peculiar to Revelation, to the divine Law, as opposed to all merely human laws, is care for the improvement of belief, i.e., for spreading right opinions about "God and the angels," and for the education of men to true knowledge of all existing things.[6]

Revelation itself thus summons those to philosophizing who are suited for it; the divine Law itself commands philosophizing. The philosophy that *is free on the basis of this authorization* takes all existing things for its subject. So, like all existing things, Revelation too becomes its subject. In prophetology Revelation becomes the subject of philosophy as the *Law* given by God through a *prophet*.

If Revelation were *merely* God's miraculous act, it would simply be withdrawn from all human comprehension. Revelation is only understandable insofar as God's revelatory act is accomplished through mediating causes, insofar as it is built into Creation, into created *nature*. If it is to be *wholly* understandable, it must simply be a *natural* fact. The means through which God accomplishes the act of Revelation is the prophet; i.e., an unusual man, distinguished above all others, but, in any case, a *man*. Philosophical understanding of Revelation and philosophical grounding of the Law thus mean the explanation of prophecy out of the *nature of man*.

Maimonides could presuppose such an explanation of prophecy. The Islamic Aristotelians—the Falāsifa—had taught that prophecy is a certain perfection of human nature that the correspondingly talented man necessarily acquires through corresponding training. Maimonides accepts this teaching with the one reservation that the correspondingly talented and prepared man does not *necessarily* become a prophet. God can, as He deems, deny prophecy to such a man. Now this miraculous denial of prophecy has fundamentally the same character as the miraculous denial of the exercise of the property of seeing or the property of moving one's hand.[7] This, however, means that only the denial of prophecy is miraculous, not prophecy as such; prophecy as such is natural.[8] If, then, the correspondingly talented and prepared man does not necessarily become a prophet, it is nevertheless necessary for the prophet to be a correspondingly talented and prepared man. Prophecy is bound to certain conditions. As Maimonides teaches, adhering to the Falāsifa, these conditions are perfection of the intellect, of morals, and of the power of imagination.[9] One understands why just those conditions are necessary if one asks how prophecy is constituted in such a way that under the revelation communicated by prophets it is possible for the life of theory to be the proper perfection of man, or in such a way that what is characteristic of Revelation, as opposed to all merely human laws, can be care for the spread of right opinions about "God and the angels."

If Revelation is to communicate the fundamental truths of theory, the bearer of Revelation, the prophet, must have command of the knowledge of these truths. At least, he must *also* be a philosopher, an actual knower. The perfection of intellect, acquired through training and instruction, is a condition of prophecy.[10] Revelation, simply binding, addresses itself to all, but only some, a few, have the capacity for the theoretical life. Therefore, the truths to (and because of) which Revelation simply obligates must be communicated to the many according to their powers of comprehension. These truths must thus— at least in part—be depicted in images. The prophet must therefore be a man who, while having command of philosophical knowledge, is at the same time capable of depicting it in images. Along with perfection of understanding, perfection of the power of imagination is also a condition of prophecy.[11]

The process of knowledge is understood by Maimonides, as by the Falāsifa, according to the then ruling conception of the Aristotelian teachings, as the actualization of the human disposition to understand (the "hylic intellect") by the extrahuman, superhuman "Active Intellect," which there is the nethermost of the incorporeal intelligences. The Active Intellect, for its part, is determined in its being and working by God. In the case of prophetic knowledge, the Active Intellect's influence on human intellect does not suffice. Since the prophet also and especially must make himself understood by the many and thus must speak in images, the Active Intellect must in his case also influence the power of imagination. We now have collected the elements that are united in Maimonides' definition of prophecy. That definition says: "According to its essence, prophecy is an emanation that emanates from God, mediated by the Active Intellect, first upon the power of intellect and then upon the power of imagination."[12]

Since in the case of prophecy, not only the intellect (as in the case of philosophical knowledge) but also the power of imagination is influenced by the Active Intellect, prophecy is, as directly following his definition of prophecy Maimonides explains: "the highest stage of man and the most extreme perfection that can be found in the human race." Even on this ground, the prophet is unconditionally *superior* to the philosopher, and all the more to all other men. He is, however, also superior to the philosopher in his own realm, as a knower. He can know *directly*, without "premises and conclusions," what all other men can only know indirectly. Accordingly, he has command over insights that the man who only knows philosophically is not capable of reaching.[13] Thus it becomes understandable that, in respect to the central question whose scientific answer man is incapable of giving (the question of whether the world is eternal or created), Maimonides can instruct the philosopher to follow the prophet.[14] In his philosophizing, the philosopher can orient himself according to the prophet because the prophet has command over insights that are not accessible to mere philosophical knowledge.

The superiority of the prophet over the philosopher now, however, comes into question through the fact with which this superiority first emerged: the participation of the power of imagination in the act of his knowledge. One does not exaggerate very much if one says that the whole *Guide of the Perplexed* is devoted to a critique of the power of imagination. Above all, the discussions of the first part—whose purpose is securing the purity of the concept of God and combating all conceptions that call into question the absolute unity of God—direct themselves against the imaginative understanding of Scripture. The power of imagination is precisely *opposed* to the intellect; it only grasps the individual, not the general. In its activity it can in no way free itself from matter and thus can never recognize a Form; that is why one should pay no attention to it at all. It necessarily impairs the activity of the intellect; liberation from its influence is an indispensable condition of true knowledge. [15] Under these circumstances, it seems only consequent for Spinoza, polemicizing against Maimonides, to say that whoever is distinguished by an especially strong power of imagination (as were the prophets, according to Maimonides' and Spinoza's assertion) is especially ill-equipped to achieve pure knowledge, and for Spinoza to deny therefore that the prophets had more than a vulgar knowledge.[16] But this "consequence" is so obvious that it would not have escaped Maimonides had it really been a consequence of his teaching.

At first it must be established that the suspicion against the power of imagination, the denigration of the power of the imagination, is sustained in Maimonides' prophetology. In line with this teaching, the highest stage of prophecy, the prophecy of Moses, is distinguished precisely because the power of imagination does *not* participate in it.[17] Establishing this, though, does not appear to have gained very much, because in any case the "ordinary" prophets (all the prophets except Moses), despite and even because of the participation of the power of imagination in their knowledge, are supposed to be superior to the philosophers. The problem thus remains of how the participation of the power of imagination can be the basis of a superiority. But in any case, this much follows: the ordinary prophets' knowledge stands in the middle between Moses' knowledge, which is free of the participation of the power of imagination, and the philosophers' knowledge, which is just as free of the participation of the power of imagination. Therefore, the distinction between the greatest prophet and the philosophers can be determined without any regard to the power of imagination. This distinction comprehends the distinction between Moses and the rest of the prophets and the distinction between the rest of the prophets and the philosophers. Therefore, it is from this deeper distinction that the difference between the rest of the prophets and the philosophers can be understood and with it the possibility, at first a paradoxical one, that the participation of the power of the imagination is the basis for the superiority of the prophets over the philosophers. We thus have to ask how, according to Maimonides' teachings, Moses' knowledge distinguishes itself from the philosophers' knowledge.

The natural representative of the philosophers is *the* philosopher, Aristotle. Now it holds of Aristotle that everything he says about the sublunary world is undoubtedly true, while his assertions about the upper world, especially about the incorporeal intelligences, are only in part probable and in part even wrong.[18] What holds for Aristotle holds all the more for other non-prophetic men. Man can only know the sublunary world, the world that surrounds him, lies before his eyes, and is known to him, the world to which he belongs, *his* world. Only this lower world is directly accessible to him; his knowledge of the upper world remains necessarily fragmentary and doubtful. The designations "upper" and "lower" not only express a spatial relationship but at the same time a distinction of rank. The upper world is the higher world by rank; it is inaccessible to human knowledge not just because of its spatial distance but also because of its high rank. The lower world is the world of becoming and decaying. The ground of all becoming and decaying, of all deficiency in general, is matter. Matter, our determination by it and our adhesion to it, is the reason we can only inadequately[19] fulfill our proper and highest determination, the knowledge of the upper world, "of God and the angels."[20] The highest knowledge is secret from us; only occasionally does the truth shine forth to us so that we opine it is day; forthwith, however, it is withdrawn from our view by matter, and by our life, which adheres to matter. We live in a deep, dark night that is only occasionally illuminated by lightning bolts. From this image, the hierarchy of men can be depicted. For one, lightning bolt after lightning bolt beams forth with only small intervals between them, so that for him night almost becomes day. This stage of almost continuous life in the light is the stage of Moses. For others, the lightning bolts follow only at great intervals; this is the stage of the rest of the prophets.[21] And finally, there are men for whom lightning only beams forth once in the whole night. To this stage belong those of whom it is said: "They prophesied and did not continue." Then there is a class of men for whom the darkness has never been illuminated by a lighning bolt, but only by polished bodies in the manner of certain stones that shine in the night. And even this light does not shine continuously for us (!), but it shines and forthwith disappears. Finally, there are men who see no light at all. This last class is the many, who know nothing. The first three classes comprehend all the prophets, from the highest to the lowest. Then the class of those for whom the darkness is only illuminated by a little— and that a borrowed, mediated—light must be the class of the philosophers. By the mediation of their knowledge of the upper world, the philosophers distinguish themselves from the prophets, who have command over a more or less great direct knowledge of the upper world.[22] The ordinary prophets distinguish themselves from Moses in that they do not live, like him, continually in the light, but the lightning bolts only beam forth for them at greater intervals.

In the *Mishneh Torah*,[23] Maimonides expresses this distinction as follows: the ordinary prophets do not have command over prophetic knowledge at any time, whenever they want, whereas prophecy comes over Moses whenever he wants. Moses does not need to prepare himself for prophecy like the rest of the prophets; he *is* always prepared. A further distinction is made in the cited passage: the rest of the prophets are in fear, confusion, and excitement during their prophetic knowing, while Moses receives his prophecy in calm and firmness. If we think back to the parable of the deep, dark night and the illuminating lightning bolts, we understand what Maimonides is pointing to in speaking of the confusion of the ordinary prophets. The all too bright, unaccustomed light of direct knowledge confuses the ordinary prophets and makes them anxious. And if the philosophers distinguish themselves from the prophets in that they do not know this confusion and anxiety, they simply owe this "advantage" to the circumstance that only the "small light" of indirect knowledge shines for them. The prophet is confused *because* he sees more, and more directly, than the philosopher.

From this it now can also be understood why the participation of the power of imagination in prophetic knowledge can be the basis for the superiority of the prophet over the philosophers. *Because* the prophet knows more, and more directly, than the philosopher, because he is blinded by the all too bright, unaccustomed light, he therefore represents in images what has become known to him. What has become known imbues him *wholly*, grasps him wholly, and therefore also grasps his power of imagination. Because the power of imagination is wholly grasped, wholly put in service "from above," it cannot *disturb* philosophical knowledge as it does with the rest of men. The prophet does not represent "God and the angels" in images, and thus corporeally, because he *holds* them to be corporeal (only the unknowing do this) but because he has known them directly in their incorporeality and thus has known them more clearly than the philosopher. His understanding of the upper world is precisely *not* imaginative *understanding*; the depiction of the known in images is the consequence of his superabundant knowledge. For the prophet, the participation of the power of imagination truly is not because his knowledge lags behind philosophical knowledge but because of an infinite advantage over the latter. The prophet stands in *direct* relation to the upper world.

We now have the possibility of understanding the third condition of prophecy—perfection of morals. The express emphasis on this condition could at first seem superflous; after all, moral perfection seems an indispensable condition of intellectual perfection. Nevertheless, experience shows that there are men of intellectual perfection who are still ruled by the desire for the pleasures of the senses and thus are far removed from moral perfection. How is this fact to be understood? An intellectually perfect man who is not a prophet is doubtless *also* imbued with the desire for knowledge, and he can fulfill this desire only insofar as he makes himself free from the desire for the lower pleasures. But he is not *wholly* imbued with the desire for knowledge. Man is hindered in the knowledge of the upper world by being chained to *his* world, by his corporeality and sensuality. Usually he is wholly absorbed with his pondering and aspiring in this world. His dreams show that this is so. While he dreams, man has in a certain manner loosed himself from the surrounding world, but what he dreams is wholly determined by his worldly pondering and aspiring. A man can thus very well have a strong desire for knowledge, and hence, if he is correspondingly talented and schooled, he can arrive at intellectual perfection. But his most secret pondering and aspiring, as it shows itself in dreams, does not therefore have to be directed to knowledge. It is thus not sufficient for man to free himself of sense perception; he must also free himself of all sensual desire, of all adherence to the world. In the concealed depths of his heart he must want nothing else than the knowledge of "God and the angels." If he does this, if he *thus "dreams"* of nothing else than of this knowledge, then, presupposing that he is a man of perfect power of imagination and of perfect understanding, he will, in the condition of detachment from the material world—in dream and vision— only perceive divine things, only see God and his angels.[24]

We summarize: the prophet is a man of perfect understanding and of perfect power of imagination who is wholly ruled by the desire for knowledge of the upper world. Only such a man can stand in *direct* connection with the upper world, can know "God and the angels" directly. This knowledge, which is superior to all other human knowledge, qualifies him to be a *teacher* of men, and a teacher *also* of *philosophers*. The fact that his power of imagination is also wholly grasped by knowledge of the upper world especially qualifies him to give a depiction of his knowledge in images, and therefore to teach the *many*.

III

The part of Maimonides' prophetology we have discussed so far can be understood univocally in itself. The actual difficulties concern the part that is now to be discussed, both taken by itself and also in connection with the first part. We begin with a provisional orientation about the subject of the still unexamined part of Maimonides' prophetology.

As yet, the power of imagination has only confronted us in its function of depicting in images the insights of intellect. This function of the power of imagination has as its necessary condition the actualization of the intellect. Aside from this consequent activity of the power of imagination in prophetic knowledge, there still exists another—at least one other—independent activity of that power, whose dependence on the activity of the intellect is not evident from the beginning. *Knowledge of the future* is based on this activity.

The future is not only known by prophets but also, even if in a more limited way, by ordinary men in truthful dreams. In sleep, when the senses rest, the power of imagination is free to receive the emanation of the Active Intellect; in this way the future is made known to men. The activity of the power of imagination in truthful dreams is distinguished only by degree from its activity in the prophetic knowledge of the future. The power of imagination of the prophet is of the greatest possible perfection, but it is the same power in him as in all men. The truthful dream comes about through the influence of the Active Intellect on the power of imagination, just as philosophy becomes real through the influence of the Active Intellect on (human) intellect. If the Active Intellect works on intellect *and* the power of imagination, prophecy comes about.[25] The question is whether Maimonides means that intellect and the power of the imagination participate in the prophet's knowledge of the future[26] as they do in the depiction of theoretical insights in images. This is not the only question to remain unanswered by Maimonides; he also does not answer the more fundamental question: How is it to be understood that such basically different activities as the depiction of theoretical insights in images and the knowledge of the future are jointly characteristic of the prophet? We want to try to answer this question, taking into consideration Maimonides' *sources*. To justify this procedure, we must clarify the general relationship of Maimonides' prophetology to the prophetology of the Falāsifa.

Maimonides himself says that his teaching is in accord with the Falāsifa's teaching—except for *one* point. This one point is the reservation that prophecy, which came to be on the basis of fundamentally determined conditions, did not, as the Falāsifa assert, necessarily come to be; despite the fulfillment of all conditions, it could be denied as God deemed fit. Maimonides' reservation thus does not concern the essence and the natural conditions of prophecy. According to the Falāsifa's teaching, the conditions of prophecy are perfection of the understanding, of morals, and of the power of imagination. Maimonides teaches the same thing. According to Maimonides, prophecy, according to its essence, is an emanation out of God which, by means of the Active Intellect, streams forth first to the intellect and afterward to the power of imagination. The Falāsifa already taught the same thing before him. Thus, in the decisive explanation of prophecy, Maimonides, according to his explicit assurance, is in accord with the Falāsifa.[27]

Above all, the writings of Alfarabi and Avicenna come under consideration as Maimonides' sources. The most comprehensive and extensive depiction of *Alfarabi's* prophetology is found in his text, *The Virtuous City*;[28] in what follows, we will consider only this depiction. Alfarabi speaks of prophecy in two different passages of *The Virtuous City*. He treats a different kind of prophecy in each of these passages, without explicitly saying so, to be sure. The kind treated first is based solely on the power of imagination; the second is based on intellect and the power of imagination. The power of imagination has three functions: it protects the impressions of the things of the senses, it combines these impressions, and finally and above all, it reproduces the things of the senses.[29] In general it is dependent—and thus especially for its reproductive functions as well—on receiving material from somewhere else. Waking, it receives material above all from sense perception. But since it then stands in the service of other powers of the soul, its independent activity cannot unfold itself. It comes to this unfolding in sleep, when the senses and the intellect rest. Then it reproduces what the senses have perceived. Occasionally it digests, in a corresponding manner, what the intellect brings to it—in a corresponding manner, since, because it is not capable of receiving the things of the intellect as such, it imitates them by making them sensory. Thus it depicts the things of the intellect that are of the highest perfection (like the first cause, the immaterial existences, the heavens) by the most perfect things of the senses (by things of beautiful appearance). In just the same way, it digests in a corresponding manner what is offered by the other powers of the soul (the power of nourishment, and so forth).[30] The power of imagination can also receive content from the Active Intellect. In that case, it takes over the function of the (human) intellect.

There are two kinds of intellect: the theoretical, which knows the things of the intellect, and the practical, which has to do with partial things (*particularia*). If the Active Intellect works on the power of the imagination, then it thus receives *either* things of the intellect *or* partial, and especially future, things. It necessarily makes sensory the things of the intellect; as for the partial things, it sometimes represents them as they really are, whereas in other cases it depicts them through other partial things, which are more or less like them.[31] Knowledge of the future thus comes to be in the same manner as the sensualizing conception of the things of the intellect: through the influence of the Active Intellect on the power of imagination.

There are different stages of imaginative comprehension. The lowest and most common is knowledge of the future in sleep, in the truthful dream. Higher than the truthful dreamer stands the one who, in his sleep, grasps things of the intellect in the form of images; the highest is the one who, while awake, is capable of receiving the (future) partial things as well as the images of the things of the intellect. This stage is the highest to which the power of imagination can reach and is absolutely the highest to which man can arrive by means of the power of imagination.[32]

The second kind of prophecy distinguishes itself from the first in that the actualization of the intellect, as well as the highest perfection of the power of imagination, is a condition for it. To the man who fulfills these conditions, God guarantees revelations by mediation of the Active Intellect. What emanates from God upon the Active Intellect, the Active Intellect lets emanate, first upon the intellect of the correspondingly disposed man and afterwards upon his power of imagination.[33] He becomes a philosopher through that which emanates from the Active Intellect upon the intellect of the prophet; he becomes a prophet, i.e., one who warns of the future, through that which emanates from the Active Intellect upon his power of imagination. His power of imagination must be so perfect that it can receive from the Active Intellect not only the partial things but also the things of the intellect in a sensory form.[34] The man who fulfills the given conditions is capable of communicating what he has received from the Active Intellect in a manner suited to the many.[35] This man stands on the highest stage of humanity simply,[36] in distinction to the prophet of the first kind, who only reaches the highest stage attainable by means of the power of imagination alone.

The comparison of Maimonides' prophetology with Alfarabi's results in this:[37] Maimonides denies the lower, exclusively imaginative prophecy that Alfarabi had acknowledged. Therefore, for Maimonides the highest stage of humanity and the highest stage of the power of imagination coincide in *the* prophecy, whereas Alfarabi could distinguish the highest stage of the power of imagination as such from the highest stage of humanity simply.[38] Maimonides thus only acknowledges the higher kind of prophecy as prophecy, but in regard to it he agrees extensively with Alfarabi. A merely apparent difference is that Alfarabi does not mention moral perfection as a condition of prophecy. Alfarabi's expositions about bliss show that in this matter there is full agreement between Maimonides and Alfarabi. Bliss consists of freedom from matter. It is reached directly through the actualization of the intellect; however, moral virtue is a mediating condition.[39] A real difference may be present in that Alfarabi denies the possibility of superphilosophical knowledge of the upper world by the prophet. Through the influence of the Active Intellect on his intellect, the prophet becomes a philosopher,[40] nothing other and nothing higher than a philosopher.[41] In case Maimonides teaches differently on this important point from Alfarabi, he still does not move into opposition to *the* Falāsifa; in any case, he found the teaching of the prophet's direct knowledge in *Avicenna*. According to Avicenna, the highest capacity characterizing the prophet is just the capacity for direct knowledge, which does not rest on conclusions or proofs.[42]

Avicenna teaches[43] that among men, those take precedence who have achieved intellectual and moral perfection. Among these in turn, and hence among all men, he is the most excellent who is disposed to the stage of prophecy.[44] The prophet is characterized by the following three capacities of the soul: (1) perfection of the power of imagination, (2) the capacity to work miracles, and (3) direct knowledge. The man who also has command of these three capacities in addition to intellectual and moral perfection receives revelations; he hears the word of God and sees the angels of God in visible form. There is a rank relation among the three capacities characterizing the prophet. Imaginative prophecy occupies the lowest rank; the prophecy with the power to transform matter, to work miracles stands higher; and the highest rank is occupied by the prophecy that consists of the highest perfection simply of the theoretical intellect.[45] This should not be understood as though the prophet of the highest stage also does not have command of the capacities of the prophets of the other two stages. Avicenna especially assumes the cooperation of the power of imagination in prophecy as such and thus also in the highest stage of prophecy, as shown by his definition of prophecy as such: Prophecy is hearing the word of God and seeing the angels of God in *visible* form.[46]

Thus we may say that the decisive elements of Maimonides' prophetology are found in the same context in Alfarabi, or in Avicenna, or in both.[47] The only essential element, at least in Avicenna's teaching, that is missing in Maimonides' prophetology is the teaching of the miracle-working power of the prophets. Admittedly, in his writings one can find some disparate utterances along the lines of this teaching,[48] but if one achieves clarity concerning the general tendency of his teaching about miracles, it follows that these utterances cannot be decisive. Here, too, his sources must be considered.

In Islamic philosophy, two conceptions of miracles stood opposed to each other.[49] According to the Kalām's teaching, miracles occur through God's power, not through the prophet's activity. The prophet's only relationship to the miraculous event is that he announces it in advance. The realization of the previously announced miracle is the divine confirmation of the prophecy; by this announcement, actual miracles distinguish themselves from the miracles accomplished by the saints and from works of magic. In contrast to the Kalām, the Falāsifa—basing themselves on the principle that everything that happens does not have its reason in God's unconditional, arbitrary will but must proceed from other events, under certain conditions—teach that miracles are worked, not just announced, by the prophets. Maimonides takes account of the Falāsifa's principle in teaching that miracles are in a certain sense in nature. When God created nature he instilled into it the power to bring forth miracles at a predetermined time; God lets the prophet know the time when he is to announce the relevant event, and this is the "sign" of the prophet.[50] Just like the Falāsifa, then, Maimonides denies that God intervenes according to arbitrary will into the world He created. But, on the basis of the Falāsifa, he holds firm to the Kalām's conception of the functions the prophet exercises with respect to miracles. The prophet only announces the miracle; he does not work it; it is worked by God. If the miracle is, however, worked by God and not by the prophet, then prophecy itself can depend upon God's free, miraculous act. Maimonides can therefore teach that a man who fulfills all the conditions of prophecy can nevertheless still be denied prophecy in a miraculous manner. This teaching is *the* reservation he holds against the Falāsifa's prophetology. This reservation is possible only if the miracle is not essentially worked by the prophet. Maimonides gives up the teaching of the miraculous activity of the prophets—only this element distinguishes his prophetology from that of the Falāsifa. He thereby confirms his own explanation that his prophetology only distinguishes itself in one single point from that of the Falāsifa—namely, in the cited reservation. In view of the fundamental agreement between Maimonides and the Falāsifa, we thus have a fundamental right, if Maimonides' utterances leave us unclear, to clarify the darkness of his prophetology through recourse to the corresponding teachings of the Falāsifa. Having secured this right for ourselves, we return to the question Maimonides has left unanswered. How is it to be understood that activities so fundamentally different as the depiction in images of theoretical insights and the knowledge of the future are jointly characteristic for the prophet?

If one goes back to Alfarabi's teaching, this darkness clears itself up as follows. Knowledge of the future is knowledge of partial things (*particularia*). The knowledge of partial things is a matter of the *practical* intellect. If in a truthful dream or in prophecy future things are known, the power of imagination represents the practical intellect. The knowledge of the things of understanding, whose sensory rendering is characteristic of prophecy, is a matter of the *theoretical* intellect. If in a truthful dream or in prophecy things of the intellect are known, then the power of imagination, which admittedly cannot conceive the things of the intellect as such but necessarily depicts them in images, represents the theoretical intellect.[51] That the prophet—according to Maimonides, the prophet simply, according to Alfarabi, the prophet of the higher kind—has command over the knowledge of the things of the intellect and over the knowledge of the future thus signifies that the prophet has command over both (perfect) theoretical and practical knowledge. Theoretical knowledge, however, consists of an untroubled, purely intellectual conception of the things of the intellect. The sensory depiction of the things of the intellect has nothing to do with theoretical knowledge; it has meaning only in that through it certain teachings, without which society cannot endure, are communicated to the many. If the purely intellectual "inner meaning" of the prophetic speeches transmits theoretical truths, then the imaginative "outer meaning" transmits the teachings of these speeches that are useful, especially for the improvement of the condition of human societies.[52] The participation of the power of imagination in prophetic knowledge thus has a practical intention in every case—in knowledge of the future as well as in rendering sensory the things of the intellect, which only takes place in order to lead the many. It thus becomes understandable how Maimonides can say that if the Active Intellect influences only a man's power of imagination, he becomes a politician and lawgiver or a truthful dreamer or soothsayer or magician; all these activities, called forth simply by the influence of the power of imagination and that seemingly have nothing in common with each other, have in common the essential element that they are *practical*. By contrast, if only a man's understanding is influenced by the Active Intellect, he becomes a philosopher, a *theorist*; and if his intellect as well as his power of imagination are influenced by the Active Intellect, he becomes a prophet.[53] Prophecy is thus a unification of theoretical and practical perfection (and at once an enhancement of each of these perfections above the measure reachable by the non-prophets). In the same way that the Active Intellect must influence the intellect of the prophet so that he can communicate theoretical truths to men and be a *teacher* of men, the Active Intellect must influence the power of imagination of the prophet so that he can fulfill his *practical* task. Prophecy is at once theoretical and practical; the prophet is *teacher and leader in one*.

IV

If it is necessary for prophecy to ensure that intellect and the power of imagination are jointly influenced by the Active Intellect, and if influencing only the intellect makes man into a philosopher and influencing only the power of the imagination makes him into a politician, truthful dreamer, soothsayer, or magician, this says that *the prophet is philosopher-statesman-seer-miracle-worker in one*. Now, are the practical properties "sublated" in prophecy of equal worth with each other? If one remembers the parallel in Alfarabi's *The Virtuous City* in which the prophet appears as philosopher and seer in one,[54] one might be inclined to see in divination the prophet's most outstanding practical function. Indeed, the prophet's miracle working also leads back to divination insofar as he does not participate in the miracle in any other way than by announcing it in advance. We thus have to ask whether divination or politics is the most outstanding practical function of the prophet. We sharpen the question: What is the ultimate purpose of prophecy? Why is the human race dependent on prophets?

The answer Maimonides gives to this question, although not explicitly as such, says that man is by nature a political being and,[55] in distinction to the rest of the living beings, he needs association with others by nature. On the other hand, in no species other than the human is there so great a difference, even oppositeness, in the character of individuals. Since socialization is nowhere so necessary and so difficult as it is with men, they thus need a *leader* who regulates the actions of individuals so that, in place of natural opposition, an agreement based on statute is substituted. The survival of the human race thus depends on there being individuals who have the faculty of leadership. Therefore divine wisdom, which wanted the survival of the human race, had to give this faculty to it. There are two kinds of leadership: lawgiving and ruling. The lawgiver establishes the norms for action; the ruler compels them to be followed. Ruling leadership thus always presupposes lawgiving leadership. The most original[56] kind of leadership is *lawgiving*. Lawgiving can have as its purpose perfection either of the body or of the soul; or rather, since the realization of the higher perfection has for a necessary presupposition the realization of the lower, lawgiving can limit itself to the establishment of the means serving the bodily perfections, or it can strive for the perfection of the body in the service of perfection of the soul. Perfection of the soul, or, more precisely, perfection of the intellect, is man's characteristic perfection.[57] The law that is directed toward man's characteristic perfection is a *divine law*, and its proclaimer is a *prophet*.[58] The prophet is thus the proclaimer of a law that is directed to the proper perfection of man. But the law intends to make living together possible. Therefore the prophet is the founder of a society that is directed to the proper perfection of men.

It turned out to be Maimonides' teaching that the prophet is philosopher-statesman-seer-(miracle-worker) in one. Since, then, the purpose of prophecy is the founding of a society directed toward the proper perfection of man, we may summarize that the prophet must be philosopher-statesman-seer-(miracle-worker) in one *so that* he can be the founder of a society directed to the proper perfection of man, the perfect society. If the founder of the perfect society must be a prophet, and the prophet is more than a philosopher, it is thereby said that the founding of a perfect society is not possible for a man who is only a philosopher. That is why the philosopher, too, depends on a Law given by a prophet; the philosopher, too, must obey the prophet. He would have to obey him even if his theoretical insight were no less than the prophet's; for this theoretical insight would not qualify him for lawgiving, and, as a political being, man can only live under a law.

On the way to determining the essence of the prophet—the prophet as philosopher-statesman-seer-(miracle-worker) in one as the founder of the perfect society—we came across the question of what is the purpose of prophecy. We said that Maimonides, to be sure, gives us an answer to this question, but not explicitly as such. Thus it must still be shown that Maimonides' teaching, to which we have referred, is to be looked at, in his sense, as an answer to our question. To show this, we must again return to the sources.

In his explanation of the chapter of the *Guide of the Perplexed* that deals tacitly with the purpose of prophecy (II, 40), Shemtob Falaquera introduces a parallel from the *Metaphysics* of Avicenna, which apparently is held to be the closest source for Maimonides' presentation. This parallel is only comprehensible in its whole range if one considers it in the light of Avicenna's virtually programmatic explanations about the place of prophetology in the whole of the sciences. It turns out from his treatise "On the Parts of the Sciences" that, in his view, the science that must concern itself thematically with prophecy is *politics*. It is already thereby said that the purpose of prophecy is political and that the most excellent practical function of the prophet is not divination but political leadership.[59]

In the above treatise, Avicenna begins by listing the subjects of politics: the kinds of regimes and political associations, the kind and manner of their preservation and the cause of their fall, and the manner in which the different forms of states pass over into each other. Then he continues: "whatever of this has to do with monarchy is contained in the book of Plato and Aristotle on the state; whatever of this has to do with *prophecy* and the *religious Law* is contained in both the books of both of these about the *Laws.* . . . This part of practical philosophy (namely, politics)[60] has as its subject the presence of prophecy and man's dependency with respect to this presence, its duration and its propagation in the religious law. Politics treats all religious laws together, as well as the individual religious laws, according to people and era and peculiar characters; it treats the distinction between divine prophecy and all worthless pretensions."[61] In accord with his classification of the sciences, Avicenna has treated prophecy in the concluding part of his *Metaphysics*, which is devoted to practical philosophy. To be sure, he also speaks of prophecy under psychology, but in this context he only discusses the characteristic capacities of prophets, and thus only the means and not the end and meaning of prophecy. That prophecy as such is not the theme of psychology is shown above all in the fact that the prophetic capacities are not treated in one context under psychology but in quite different places, namely, every time a power of the soul is discussed whose highest perfection is characteristic of the prophet.

The human race's dependency on prophecy is fundamentally indicated just as much by Avicenna as by Maimonides. Man is distinguished from animals by the fact that his life cannot be perfect if he lives for himself; man can only then live properly as man if he lives in society. The presence and survival of the human race depend on men living in society; society presupposes mutual traffic; traffic is not possible without the ordering of life and justice; the ordering of life is not possible without a Lawgiver; the Lawgiver must be able to talk to men and to obligate them to the ordering of life given by him; he must, then, be a man. He may not leave men to their opinions about right and wrong, for each holds what is advantageous to himself for right and what is disadvantageous to himself for wrong; accordingly, the human race depends for its survival on such a man, but that means on a *prophet*. It is therefore impossible for divine providence not to take care of this necessity. It is thus necessary that there really is (or was) a prophet. He must have qualities that other men lack, so they can surmise his superiority and he can distinguish himself from them.[62]

If this grounding of prophecy is approached from the corresponding presentations of the *Guide of the Perplexed*, at first sight one misses the sharp distinction between the divine Law, whose purpose is the proper perfection of man and whose proclaimer is the prophet, *and* the merely human law, whose purpose is only the perfection of the body and whose proclaimer is the statesman. Nevertheless, this distinction already announces itself in the passage cited (on pp. 100–101) from the treatise "On the Parts of Science."[63] There Avicenna distinguishes between the part of politics that deals with *monarchy* and the part that deals with *prophecy and religious law*. In a related context, he says that the use of *politics* consists of knowing how the social relations among human individuals must be constituted so that they help each other mutually toward the well-being of *bodies* and the preservation of the human species.[64] This utterance requires the question, by what is prophecy distinguished from all that is merely political? We allow Avicenna to answer this question himself. In a treatise devoted especially to the basis of prophecy, he says that the (prophetic) mission is the inspiration whose purpose is "the health of *both* worlds, that of (eternal) duration and that of decay, through science *and* political leadership. The messenger[65] (the prophet) is he who proclaims what, through inspiration, ... he has experienced, so that by his opinions, *the health of the world of the senses* ensues *by means of political leadership*, and (*the health*) *of the intelligible world* ensues by means of science."[66] Prophecy thus distinguishes itself from merely political leadership in that its purpose is not, like the latter's, merely the well-being of the body, the health of the world of the senses, but also the perfection of the intellect, the proper perfection of man. Thus Maimonides' teaching of the purpose of prophecy accords completely with Avicenna's teaching.

The comparison of Maimonides' teaching with Avicenna's confirms the assertion that, according to Maimonides' teaching, the prophet, as philosopher-statesman-seer-(miracle-worker) in one, is the founder of the perfect society. Avicenna characterizes the perfect society as "the excellent city," or as "the city of beautiful interchange";[67] we may say instead the ideal state. *The prophet is the founder of the ideal state.* The classic outline of the ideal state is the *Platonic* state. Avicenna refers to Plato's works of state, to the *Republic* and the *Laws* as the classic depictions of politics, just as he refers to Aristotle's *Ethics* as the classic depiction of ethics. The *Laws*, especially, are the decisive depiction of the philosophical teaching on prophecy.[68] In this context, to be sure, he also mentions Aristotle's *Politics*, but he can only have known it by name, since it was never translated into Arabic.[69] The following passage from Avicenna's *Great Metaphysics* shows the decisiveness of precisely the orientation to Plato's *Republic*: "the first intention of the Lawgiver in giving the Law must be the division of the city into three parts: the leaders, the artisans, and the guardians."[70] The prophet thus has to divine the state according to the divisions prescribed in Plato's *Republic*. The prophet is the founder of the Platonic state; the prophet fulfills what Plato demanded.[71]

The originator of this conception of prophecy seems to be *Alfarabi*. His work on Platonic politics is most plainly witnessed by the fact that he composed an "extract" or "summa" of the Platonic *Laws*.[72] We have already mentioned that Alfarabi distinguishes two kinds of prophecy (see above, pp. 91–92). It is very important to pay attention to the context in which he treats each of these kinds. He speaks of the lower prophecy in connection with psychology; he first discusses the higher prophecy after he has treated "man's need for association and mutual aid"—basically just like Avicenna and Maimonides. He indicates thereby that the higher prophecy, prophecy proper, distinguishes itself from vulgar divination of all grades by its *political* mission; prophecy proper can only be radically understood from the context of politics. Here "politics" and "political" are to be understood in Plato's sense. Alfarabi is not concerned with a state in general but with the state directed to the proper perfection of man, with the "excellent state," the ideal state. According to Alfarabi the ruler of the ideal state must be a man of perfect intellect and perfect power of imagination; he must be a man upon whom God allows Revelation to be bestowed by means of the Active Intellect.[73] In other words, the ruler of the ideal state must be a prophet-philosopher and seer in one.[74] He must have command by nature over the following qualities, among others:[75] he must love learning and learn easily; he must have a strong memory; he may not be greedy for sensual pleasures; he must love the truth and hate deception; he may not love money; and finally, he must "be firmly resolved upon the matter whose execution he deems necessary, brave upon it, daring, without fear and not of weak heart."[76] This means that the ruler of the ideal state—and only a *prophet* can be the ruler of the ideal state—must by nature have the qualities that, according to Plato's requirement, the *philosopher-kings* must have by nature.[77]

Pointing back to Plato is not just the fact that in Maimonides' and the Falāsifa's prophetology the unification of philosophy and politics is presupposed as the condition of the perfect state whose founder can only be a prophet. The understanding of how the prophet is a philosopher is also of Platonic descent. The prophet is a man who, after he has received the *revelation* (*wachy*), is able to bring men the *message* (*risāla*) that leads to the health of the world of the senses by means of political leadership and to the health of the intelligible world by means of science (see above, p. 102). Revelation is an emanation from God which, by means of the Active Intellect, grants the prophet direct knowledge of the upper world. Only the direct knowledge of the upper world, so it seems, qualifies the prophet for leading men, which is proper to him, uniting in itself politics and science. Maimonides illustrates the character of this direct knowledge by the following parable. From the outset, all men live in a deep, dark night. The night is illuminated at all only for a few men, for most of these (the philosophers) by borrowed, earthly light and for very few (the prophets) by lightning bolts from on high (see above, pp. 87 ff.). In the explanation of the passage in the *Guide of the Perplexed* in which this parable appears, Shemtob Falaquera points to a related passage in the same work (III,51). There he introduces a parallel from Alfarabi, which says the following:[78] There are three stages of men. The first is the stage of the *many*. The many know the things of the understanding only in material forms; they are like those who live in a cave and for whom the sun has never shone; they see, so to speak, only the shadows of things, never the light itself. The second stage is that of the *philosophers*; they know the things of the understanding but only indirectly, as one sees the sun in the water (what one sees in the water is only the image of the sun, not the sun in itself). The philosophers are like men who have left the cave and have gazed at the light. The third stage is the stage of the *blissful*; the men of this stage see the thing in itself; they see, as it were, the light itself. In their seeing there is absolutely nothing seeming; they themselves become the thing they see.

The relationship between the *Platonic parable of the cave* and Maimonides' parable of the deep, dark night and the lightning bolts that illuminate it, confirmed by Falaquera's reference, justifies the following assertion: Just as according to Plato the perfect state can only be realized through the philosopher who has ascended from the cave into the light, who has gazed upon the idea of the Good, so according to Maimonides and the Falāsifa, the perfect state can only be realized through the prophet for whom the night in which the human race gropes has been illuminated by lightning bolts from on high, by direct knowledge of the upper world.

V

The prophet as philosopher-statesman-seer-(miracle-worker) in one is the founder of the ideal state. The ideal state is understood according to Plato's guidance: the prophet is the founder of the Platonic state. Plato's requirement that philosophy and political power must coincide if the true state is to become real and his concept of the philosopher-king demarcate the framework that, taking account of the completed fulfillment of the factual revelation, results in the concept of prophecy of the Falāsifa and Maimonides. Understanding this prophetology thus depends on clearing up the relationship of the concept of the prophet to the Platonic concept of the philosopher-king. Ultimately, it depends on clearing up the relationship of the position of the Falāsifa to the position of Plato. The relationship of the Falāsifa and Maimonides to Plato is characterized from the very first by the fact that the former begin from an un-Platonic presupposition. For the Falāsifa and Maimonides the *fact* of Revelation is established. Thus it is established for them that a simple binding Law, a divine Law, a Law with the power of right, proclaimed by a prophet, is real. This Law authorizes them to philosophize. Philosophizing, they ask about the possibility of the real Law; they answer this question within the horizon of Platonic politics; they understand Revelation in the light of Platonic politics. From an un-Platonic presupposition—from the presupposition of Revelation—they adopt Platonic politics.

The attempt to understand the real Revelation within the horizon of Platonic politics compels alteration of the Platonic framework in respect to the real Revelation. It suffices to recall what significance the prophet's knowledge of the future (and working of miracles) has for Maimonides and the Falāsifa. The Platonic framework is only altered thereby; it is broadened to some extent, but it is not burst; it remains the spiritual bond that unifies philosophy and politics. The alteration under discussion as such implies a *critique* of Plato. This critique gets its entire weight because it can appeal to the fact of Revelation. An alteration of the Platonic project, i.e., a critique of the Platonic answer, results from the *factual* answer to the Platonic question about the true state. If the founder of the perfect society can only be a prophet, this says that founding the perfect society is not possible for the man who is only a philosopher. It is not, as Plato asserts, that the coincidence of philosophy and political power suffices for the realization of the true state; the ruler-philosopher must be *more* than a philosopher. In projecting the true state, Plato did foretell Revelation.[79] But just as only the fulfillment first teaches complete understanding of the foretelling, so the Platonic project must be altered from the perspective of the factual Revelation, the factual ideal state.

The alteration undertaken by the Falāsifa and Maimonides of the Platonic framework had already been prepared in the Hellenistic era. In this era we encounter the teaching that in the primordial age, rulers, philosophers, and seers coincided.[80] Two elements that apparently—but only apparently—have nothing in common distinguish this teaching from the Platonic concept of the philosopher-ruler: (1) the esteem for divination, and (2) the conviction that the perfect condition of mankind had been real in the prehistoric past. For this teaching too, the ideal leadership[81] is a fact, not just something to be desired. Neo-Pythagorean views prepare a further element distinguishing the Falāsifa's prophetology from Plato's teaching of the philosopher-ruler: the teaching of the prophet's miracle-working.[82] Above all, Philo prepares the teaching of the prophet's direct knowledge, which distinguishes him from the philosopher.[83]

But after all, what does it signify that the prophetology that was prepared in the Hellenistic era is finally and decisively determined by Platonic politics? Is this fact a mere curiosity? Is it solely based on or indebted to the circumstance that Plato was once held to be "the divine Plato" and that, moreover, the *Politics* of the other great, of Aristotle, remained unknown because of an odd coincidence? The dependence of the prophetology of Maimonides and the Falāsifa on Platonic politics would then be more than a curiosity and a coincidence if these men were Platonists as such, if their un-Platonic presupposition, the fact of Revelation, were fundamentally not so un-Platonic as appears at first sight. Of Maimonides, at least, Hermann *Cohen* asserted that he was a Platonist.[84] We appropriate this assertion for ourselves, although on the basis of a deliberation that wholly differs in individual things from Cohen's substantiation and that compels us to include the Falāsifa in this assertion.

At first sight the assertion that the Falāsifa and Maimonides are to be addressed as Platonists has everything against it. Likewise, insofar as something speaks for it at first, it takes away all precision and significance from just what speaks for it. For the Falāsifa's *teaching* (surely, one must at first hold to the teaching) is far more Aristotelian on the one hand and neo-Platonic on the other than it is properly Platonic. Therefore they seem to be Platonists in no other sense than that every Aristotelian and every neo-Platonist is a disciple of Plato. But Cohen did not mean his assertion in this sense. It was, after all, one of the most important concerns of his efforts in the history of philosophy to grasp the relationship of Aristotle to Plato as an irreconcilable *opposition*. Guided by this conception of Aristotle's relationship to Plato, he came to an assertion that has content solely on the basis of this presupposition; however, in view of Maimonides' apparent Aristotelianism, this assertion, on the basis of this presupposition, was paradoxical: "Maimonides was in deeper harmony with Plato than with Aristotle."[85]

Cohen understands the contrast between Platonic (Socratic) and Aristotelian philosophizing as the contrast between primary questions about the Good, the right life, the true state *and* primary interest in contemplation of existing things and the knowledge of Being.[86] But precisely if one conceives of the relationship of Plato and Aristotle in this manner, it seems necessary to characterize the Falāsifa and Maimonides as Aristotelians without reservations. In Cohen's words: "What Maimonides did not just learn from Aristotle, but wherein, with all the depth of their difference, the latter was and remained a model and a leader, is the enthusiasm for pure theory, for scientific knowledge for its own sake, and as the last absolute purpose of human existence."[87]

Cohen most penetratingly bases his paradoxical doubt of Maimonides' Aristotelianism on the lapidary sentence, "All honor to the god of Aristotle; but he is truly not the God of Israel."[88] It cannot be examined here how Cohen tries positively to show that Maimonides was a Platonist. Even less can one examine the fact that and the reason why Cohen's presentations on this point are individually untenable and that they rest on a mistaking of historical actuality. We limit ourselves to emphasizing that the insight that precedes and guides this proof remains untouched by the way in which Cohen offers the proof of his assertion and even by the untenability of this proof: the god of Aristotle is not the God of Israel; therefore no Jew as Jew can be an Aristotelian. For him, the primacy of theory cannot now or ever be the end of the matter; he cannot assert this primacy without conditions and hesitations. If he asserts it, he must limit it in some manner so that ultimately, by this limitation, he calls it into question.

Maimonides asserts without doubt the primacy of theory. But—and this is decisive—for him philosophy does not occupy the highest stage in the human race; the prophet stands higher than the philosopher. If, therefore, something can bring Maimonides' Aristotelianism into doubt, it is certainly his prophetology. The preference for the prophet over the philosopher is, to be sure, also based on the superiority of direct, prophetic knowledge over indirect, philosophical knowledge. Still, at the same time, it is based on the quality of leadership that distinguishes the prophet from the philosopher. In contrast to the philosopher, who merely knows, the prophet is teacher and leader in one. In view of the fact that Maimonides and the Falāsifa assert a preference for prophecy over philosophy, and indeed, in that they see the purpose of prophecy as the founding of the ideal state, they may be addressed as Platonists in Cohen's sense. That the prophetology of these philosophers must also be characterized as Platonic according to its historical descent, and in what sense, is shown previously.

Under these circumstances, however, how can it be understood that, leaving aside their prophetology, the Falāsifa and Maimonides follow Aristotle more than Plato? The Platonic question about the true state requires a detour (cf. *Republic*, 435d and 504b) on which must be asked, among other things, what the soul is, what its parts are, what science is, and what that which is, is. Thus, in the Platonic intention, everything that Aristotle asks about—but which Aristotle no longer asks about in terms of the one question about the Good—must also be asked about. And not only that: Plato teaches no less decidedly than Aristotle that bliss and the proper perfection of man consist of pure contemplation and intellect. The fundamental difference between Plato and Aristotle shows itself solely in the way in which they *stand toward* theory as the highest perfection of man. Aristotle frees it wholly; rather, he leaves it in its natural freedom. By contrast, Plato *does not permit* the philosophers "what is now permitted to them," namely, the life in philosophizing or lingering in the contemplation of truth. He *"compels"* them to care for the others and to guard them so that the state will be a state in reality, a true state (*Republic*, 519d–520c). The philosopher who has *raised* himself above the world of the senses in the contemplation of the beautiful, just, and good as such, and lives and *wants* to live in contemplation, is brought *back* into the state, *bound* back to the state, through the founder of the state's command, which first considers the order of the whole and not the happiness of the parts. The philosopher also stands as such under the state; he is responsible before the state; he is not absolutely sovereign. What Plato *required*—that philosophy stand under a higher court, under the state, under the *Law*—is *fulfilled* in an era that believes in Revelation. With all freedom in pursuing knowledge, the philosophers of this era are at every moment conscious of their responsibility for the Law[89] and before the Law. They justify their philosophizing before the forum of the Law; they derive from the Law their *authorization* to philosophize as a legal *obligation* to philosophize.[90] The Platonism of these philosophers is given with their *situation*, with their factual standing under the Law. Because they stand factually under the Law, they admittedly no longer need, like Plato, to *search* for the Law, for the state, to *ask* after it. The binding and simply perfect order of human life is *given* to them through a prophet. They are therefore authorized by the Law, free to philosophize in Aristotelian freedom. *Therefore* they can Aristotelize. Cohen states it: Maimonides "underestimated the danger that lay in the depreciation of ethics in Aristotle. Also, he could the more easily overlook the danger from his standpoint because he of course saw the value of ethics secured in his religion."[91] Because for Maimonides and the Falāsifa the Law is *given*, it is therefore not the leading and first theme of their philosophizing. Therefore the metaphysical themes take up a so much broader space in their writing than the moral-political ones. However, as philosophers they must indeed try to *understand* the given Law. This understanding is made possible for them by Plato and only by Plato.

NOTES

Introduction

1. "Irrationalism" is only a variety of modern rationalism, which is "irrational" enough itself.

2. Compare, for example, Spinoza's justification of his antinomianism by recourse to the sentence that man is in the hand of God as clay is in the hand of the potter; see my book, *Spinoza's Critique of Religion*, tr. E.M. Sinclair (New York: Schocken Books, 1965), p. 204. The assertion made in the text is meant in a more important sense than might appear at first; it is to be extended to the philosophical tradition and implies that for the Enlightenment, to the extent that it is more than a restoration of older positions, it is essential to make extremes of the tradition (or the polemic against extremes of the tradition) into the foundation of a position wholly incompatible with the tradition. The intention of the Enlightenment was the rehabilitation of the natural through the denial (or limitation) of the supernatural; its achievement, however, was the discovery of a new "natural" foundation, which is anything but natural, but rather is the residue, as it were, of the "supernatural." By the beginning of modernity, the extreme possibilities and demands that had been discovered, out of the natural and the typical, by the originators of the religious as well as the philosophical tradition had become self-evident; in that sense they had become "natural." Consequently, they are no longer considered extremes in need of a radical explication; instead, they themselves serve as a "natural" foundation for the negation or reinterpretation not just of the supernatural but also and precisely of the natural and the typical. In contrast to ancient and medieval philosophy, which understands the extreme on the basis of the typical, modern philosophy, in its source

and in all cases that it does not reinstate older teachings, understands the typical on the basis of the extreme. In that way the "trivial" questions of the essence of virtue and whether it can be taught are ignored, and the extreme ("theological") virtue of love becomes the "natural" ("philosophical") virtue; in that way, the critique of the natural ideal of courage is "radicalized." The founder of the philosophical tradition made that critique in connection with his discovery of the extreme ideal of knowledge, an ideal that therefore could not be realized during life on earth. (See Plato, *Protagoras*, 349d, and *Laws*, 630c.) The virtuous character of courage thus continued to be recognized. In the "radicalized" critique of the natural ideal of courage, the virtuous character of courage as such is formally denied. In that way too, the extreme case of the right of necessity is made into the foundation of natural right; in that way the polemic against the extreme possibility of miracles becomes the foundation of the "idealistic" shift in philosophy. That natural foundation that was intended by the Enlightenment but that precisely the Enlightenment itself buried can only be made accessible if the Enlightenment's battle against "prejudices"—a battle that has been prosecuted above all by empiricism and by the modern discipline of history—is carried appropriately to the end. The enlightened critique of the tradition must be radicalized, as it was by Nietzsche, into a critique of the principles of the tradition (the Greek as well as the biblical); thereby the original understanding of these principles may again become possible. The "historicization" of philosophy is therefore, and only therefore, justified and necessary. Only the history of philosophy makes possible the ascent out of the second, "unnatural" cave (into which we have fallen, less through the tradition than through the tradition of the polemic against the tradition), into the first, "natural" cave that Plato's image depicts, and the ascent from which, to the light, is the original meaning of philosophizing.

3. We entirely pass over here that even Cohen and Rosenzweig did not establish the original, non-"internalized" meaning of the basic assertions of the tradition.

4. As for Martin Buber's reservations, cf. Rosenzweig's argument with him, which is reprinted in *Zweistromland* (Berlin: 1926), pp. 48ff.

5. The first writings of Rosenzweig (*Hegel und der Staat*, Munich and Berlin: R. Oldenbourg, 1920) as well as of Ernst Simon (*Ranke und Hegel*, Munich and Berlin: R. Oldenbourg, 1928) are devoted to the argument with Hegel.

6. This remark also refers to by far the most significant critique of the Enlightenment that came to light in the course of the return movement: Cohen's critique of Spinoza's theological-political tractate. I provisionally direct attention to my essay "Cohens Analyse der Bibelwissenschaft Spinozas," *Der Jude*, v. viii (1924), pp. 295–314.

7. Lessing, at the beginning of "Gedanken über die Heernhuter," *Gesammelte Schriften* (Berlin: Aufbau-Verlag, 1956), v. 7, p. 185.

8. Cf. here and following Strauss, *Spinoza's Critique of Religion*, pp. 37ff., p. 86, pp. 107–108, pp. 142ff., pp. 204ff., and pp. 209ff.

9. After a freedom, won and legitimized dubiously enough, had become a self-evident possession, one could allow oneself to wish to understand the tradition better than it had understood itself and thereby to hold it at bay by an ambiguous "reverence." There is a contemptuous indignation at the Enlightenment's mockery that is the correlative of this "reverence"; but this indignation is separated from the zealous indignation of Orthodoxy by the same distance that separates the aforementioned synthesis from Orthodoxy; mockery does much more justice to Orthodoxy than this later "reverence."

10. Herein lie the grounds for the fact that the Enlightenment could prove only the unknowability of miracles, not their impossibility, and that, as far as it understood itself, it could only want to prove this.

11. Cf. on this last point Nietzsche, *Beyond Good and Evil* (tr. Walter Kaufmann, New York: Vintage, 1966), aphorism 9.

12. The new probity is something other than the old love of truth; by speaking of the "intellectual conscience," "one means the 'inner' rule of science over man, and not just any science but modern science." (G. Krüger, *Philosophie und Moral in der Kantischen Kritik* [Tübingen: 1931], p. 9, fn. 2). The pristine open-mindedness that characterizes this probity is "the pristine open-mindedness of not being partial in transcendent ideals" (K. Löwith, "Max Weber und Karl Marx," *Archiv für Sozialwissenschaft und Sozialpolitik*, vol. 67, [1932], p. 72ff.). This conception of probity recalls the definition of critique: "Critique . . . has for its essence the negation of the supernatural." Gratry has objected to this: "The essence of critique is attentiveness" (A. Gratry, *Les Sophistes et la Critique* [Paris: 1864], p. 9). The opposition between probity and love of truth can be understood in the sense of this objection. The open confession that one is an atheist and the determined intention to draw all the consequences therefrom—especially rejection, with all its implications, such as the belief in progress, of that half-theism that was the dogmatic and dishonest presupposition of the post-Enlightenment synthesis—is doubtless more

honest than all reconciliations and syntheses. But if one makes an admittedly unprovable atheism into a positive, dogmatic presupposition, then the probity that is thereby expressed is obviously something other than the love of truth.

Chapter 1

1. Julius Guttmann, *Die Philosophie des Judentums* (Munich: 1933). (References to this work will be taken from *Philosophies of Judaism* [New York: Schocken Books, 1973]. This translation, by David W. Silverman, works both from the original German and the revised, Hebrew version. Wherever my translation of Strauss's citations differs from Silverman's, the difference will be indicated in the notes in brackets—Trans.)

2. Guttmann, *Philosophies of Judaism*, p. 4. [Silverman has "from a methodological point of view, the distinctiveness of religion." It should be noted that Strauss put page references for this and Guttmann's other cited work in the text in parentheses after quotations. All such references here appear in the notes.]

3. Julius Guttmann, *Religion und Wissenschaft im Mitteralterlichen und im Modernen Denken* (Berlin: 1922), pp. 66ff. (Reprinted in *Selected Writings of Julius Guttmann*, ed. Steven Katz [New York: Arno Press, 1980]).

4. Guttmann, *Religion und Wissenschaft*, p. 69.

5. Guttmann, *Religion und Wissenschaft*, p. 65.

6. Guttmann, *Religion und Wissenschaft*, p. 70.

7. The other crucial problem for the philosophy of culture is the fact of the political. (Cf. my comments on Carl Schmitt, *Der Begriff des Politischen*, in *Spinoza's Critique of Religion*, pp. 331ff.) If "religion" and "politics" are *the* facts that transcend "culture," or, to speak more precisely, are the *original* facts, then the radical critique of the concept of "culture" is possible only in the form of a "theological-political treatise." Of course, if it were not to lead again to laying the foundations of "culture," it would have to have precisely the opposite tendency of those theological-political treatises of the seventeenth century, especially those of Hobbes and Spinoza. The first condition for this would admittedly be that these seventeenth century works no longer be understood, as they hitherto have almost always been, within the horizons of the philosophy of culture.

8. [I have translated *"ursprünglich"* as "original" throughout. The reader should note that its meaning in this context and the following is "primordial" rather than "novel."]

9. Guttmann, *Philosophies of Judaism*, p. 4. ["... earlier periods did not attempt to differentiate between the methods of philosophy and religion, but sought to reconcile the contents of their teachings."]

10. Guttmann, *Philosophies of Judaism*, p. 4. ["Philosophy was thus made subservient to religion, and philosophical material borrowed from outside was treated accordingly" (p. 63). "Dependent in many respects upon ancient traditions, and productive only insofar as it [medieval philosophy] reworked and continued traditional speculations, it found here a new sphere of problems for investigation. Its recasting of traditional metaphysical ideas was due to the necessity of adapting ancient metaphysics to the personalistic religion of the Bible."]

11. Guttmann, *Philosophies of Judaism*, pp. 53–54.

12. Guttmann, *Philosophies of Judaism*; cf. pp. 30f., pp. 119ff., pp. 147ff., and pp.186f. [The corresponding place in the German text, also pp. 186f., shows Strauss's point much more clearly]; see also p. 194, pp. 198ff., p. 206, and pp. 273–274. Following Guttmann's presentation, the most important exception is the teaching of Saadia, which, moreover, "adheres to the essential contents of traditional Jewish religious ideas" (p. 83). But leaving aside that Saadia's teaching of attributes, "pursued to its last consequences," leads to a neo-Platonic and thus an essentially unbiblical concept of God (cf. pp. 78–79 and pp. 84–85), the thought of Saadia is "still primitive and unripe" (p. 76: ["characteristic of immature thinking"]). The actual conflict between the Bible and philosophy takes place only after the rise of Aristotelianism.

13. Guttmann, *Philosophies of Judaism*; cf. p. 331.

14. Guttmann, *Philosophies of Judaism*, p. 319. ["The teleological metaphysics of Aristotelianism could compromise with revealed religion"]; cf. also p. 155.

15. Guttmann, *Philosophies of Judaism*, p. 12. ["This also explains why, in the later history of monotheism, periods of intense 'personalistic' piety tended toward a mechanistic concept of nature."]

16. Guttmann, *Philosophies of Judaism*, p. 141.

17. Guttmann, *Philosophies of Judaism*, p. 332.

18. Guttmann, *Philosophies of Judaism*, p. 332.

19. Guttmann, *Philosophies of Judaism*, p. 344.

20. Guttmann, *Philosophies of Judaism*, pp. 5f., 13–14.

21. Guttmann, *Philosophies of Judaism*, p. 396. ["Despite the fact that the medieval thinkers were, in their total personalities, far more deeply rooted in the tradition and substance of Jewish life, and that belief in the divine authority of revelation was self-evident to them,

the modern thinkers, in their theoretical explanation of Judaism, upheld with greater staunchness the true meaning of its central religious doctrines."]

22. Guttmann, *Philosophies of Judaism*, p. 416. [The English version concludes with an additional section on the thought of Franz Rosenzweig.]

23. Guttmann, *Philosophies of Judaism*, p. 401. ["While theoretical reason is forever bound to the sphere of appearances, practical reason alone can elevate us to the sphere of intelligible being; it can affirm the absolute reality of the existence of God, freedom, and immortality. But from Cohen's standpoint, this metaphysical significance can no longer be allowed to religious representations."]

24. Guttmann, *Philosophies of Judaism*, p. 415. Cf. also pp. 405–406.

25. Guttmann, *Religion und Wissenschaft*, p. 68.

26. Guttmann, *Religion und Wissenschaft*, p. 72.

27. [This passage does not appear in the English version. In adding the Rosenzweig section, Guttmann took what was the concluding paragraph in the original German edition and made it the first paragraph of the Rosenzweig section, which begins on page 416 of the English translation. However, there is a change. In place of the words Strauss cites, there is: "despite the shifting of philosophical interests brought about by time and the inward life of the Jewish people."]

28. Friedrich Gogarten, *Wider die Ächtung der Autorität* (Jena: E. Diederichs, 1936), p. 41f.

29. Friedrich Gogarten, *Politische Ethik* (Jena: E. Diederichs, 1932), p. 103 (the emphasis is mine).

30. Guttmann, *Philosophies of Judaism*, p. 7.

31. Guttmann, *Philosophies of Judaism*, pp. 402–403.

32. Franz Rosenzweig, to whom I told this story, later published it in his notes to his translations of Judah Halevi. [The Boreh Olam is the creator of the world.]

33. To illuminate the position of the philosophy of existence toward Revelation, we point again to Gogarten, who explicitly denies "that there is one word that God says to man directly." *Theologische Tradition und theologische Arbeit* (Leipzig: J.C. Hinrichs, 1927), p. 12, fn. 2. Cf. also my *Spinoza's Critique of Religion*, pp. 295–296 [note 229 to text on p. 179].

34. [The English text runs 451 pages, before bibliography and footnotes; the section on medieval Jewish philosophy referred to by Strauss runs 271 pages.]

35. Guttmann, *Philosophies of Judaism*, p. 4. Cf. also p. 14, pp. 35–36, p. 48.

36. Guttmann, *Philosophies of Judaism*, p. 278. ["The formal acknowledgment of the authority of Revelation was also a self-evident assumption for the most radical thinkers of the Jewish Middle Ages, insofar as they wanted to be considered Jews."]

37. Guttmann, *Philosophies of Judaism*, p. 4. ["The distinctiveness of biblical religion is due to its ethical conception of the personality of God."]

38. Guttmann, *Religion und Wissenschaft*, pp. 63–67.

39. Guttmann, *Philosophies of Judaism*, p. 7. ["The personalist character of biblical religion stands in the most radical contrast to another, basically impersonal, form of spiritual and universal religion, which underlies all mysticism and pantheism. Whatever the significant differences between mysticism and pantheism . . . ."]

40. Guttmann, *Philosophies of Judaism*; cf. p. 158 and p. 201.

41. Guttmann, *Religion und Wissenschaft*, p. 65.

42. Guttmann, *Religion und Wissenschaft*, p. 66.

43. [Here *"originale"* is used and clearly means "novel."]

44. Guttmann, *Religion und Wissenschaft*, p. 3.

45. Guttmann takes these objections into account by his now rather more cautious, if in principle unchanged, formulation: "For it was in the philosophical explanation of religion that medieval philosophy was at its most original. Dependent in many respects upon ancient traditions, and productive only insofar as it reworked and continued traditional speculations, it found here a new sphere of problems for investigation. Its recasting of traditional metaphysical ideas was due to the necessity of adapting ancient metaphysics to the personalistic religion of the Bible." *Philosophies of Judaism*, p. 63.

46. [M. Rémi Brague suggests that *"Überlegenheit"* is a misprint of *"Unterlegenheit"* and thus should be translated as "inferiority of medieval to modern philosophy."]

47. Guttmann, *Philosophies of Judaism*, p. 330. ["Of his two religio-philosophical works, *Phaedon* and *Morgenstunden* . . ."]

48. Guttmann, *Philosophies of Judaism*, p. 63. ["Its recasting of traditional metaphysical ideas. . ."]

49. Guttmann, *Philosophies of Judaism*; cf., for example, p. 79, pp. 113–114, p. 118, and pp. 139–140.

50. Guttmann, *Philosophies of Judaism*, p. 63 [". . . was due to the necessity of adapting ancient metaphysics to the personalistic religion of the Bible."]

51. Guttmann, *Philosophies of Judaism*, p. 63.

52. Maimonides, *The Guide of the Perplexed*, tr. Shlomo Pines (Chicago: University of Chicago, 1963), I, 31, p. 67. [The italics are Strauss's.]

53. The modern Enlightenment's struggle against "prejudices" rests upon a radicalization of this insight. On the historical character of the concept of "prejudice," cf. my *Spinoza's Critique of Religion*, pp. 133ff., pp. 178ff., and p. 252.

54. Levi ben Gerson, *Milḥamot ha-shem* (Leipzig: 1866), p. 7. The expression of Maimonides cited above is naturally not his last word on the significance of Revelation for philosophy. Cf. text, p. 44f.

55. Guttmann, *Philosophies of Judaism*, p. 278. ["Insofar as they wanted to be considered Jews." The italics are Strauss's.]

56. ["*Selbstverständlich*." The word is occasionally also translated as "obviously," or "of course."]

57. [The German reads "*offenbaren, eindeutigen, einfachen Befehl*," thus alluding both to Revelation (*Offenbarung*) as manifest and to the unity of the God who gives, literally, a "one-meaning, one-fold command."]

58. See text, p. 61ff.

59. Guttmann, *Religion und Wissenschaft*, p. 12.

60. Guttmann, *Philosophies of Judaism*, p. 63.

61. Guttmann, *Philosophies of Judaism*, p. 65. [Silverman adds the word "only."]

62. Guttmann, *Philosophies of Judaism*, pp. 62–63. Cf. also p. 155.

63. Guttmann, *Philosophies of Judaism*, p. 63. [Silverman translates the last sentence: "Even the modern Enlightenment of the eighteenth century, insofar as it maintains the idea of revelation, views the relationship between religion and revelation in fundamentally the same manner." Guttmann's original speaks of "*das Verhältnis von Vernunft und Offenbarung*," i.e., reason and Revelation. Also, however, Guttmann's original has "*Offenbarungsgedanken*," which Silverman properly translates as "the idea of Revelation," but Strauss apparently misquotes the word as "*Offenbarungsglauben*," which I have translated "belief in Revelation."]

64. Guttmann, *Religion und Wissenschaft*, p. 29.

65. See the "*Gegensätze*" to "Das Erste Wolfenbüttler Fragment," *Gesammelte Schriften* (Berlin: Aufbau-Verlag, 1956), v. 7, pp. 816f.

66. Guttmann, *Philosophies of Judaism*, p. 63.

67. Guttmann, *Philosophies of Judaism*, p. 70. ["The required supplements are mere legal technicalities. . . ."]

68. Guttmann, *Philosophies of Judaism;* see especially p. 200.

69. Maimonides, *Guide,* I, 71, pp. 175f., II, 16, pp. 293ff.; II, 17, pp. 294ff.; II, 22–25, pp. 317–330. In Guttmann's *Philosophies of Judaism,* see p. 169.

70. Maimonides, *Guide,* I, 31–32, pp. 65–70; III, 8–9, pp. 430–437. Cf. also the letter to Rabbi Ḥisdai (*Kobez Teshuvot ha-Rambam ve-Iggerotav,* ed. A. Lichtenberg [Leipzig: 1859], II, 23a).

71. Maimonides, *Guide,* Introduction, pp. 15f.; and II, 38, pp. 376ff. In Guttmann, *Philosophies of Judaism,* cf. pp. 156f. and p. 172. Guttmann, supported by the relevant text in the introduction to the *Guide,* I, asserts that there is only a *gradual* distinction between the "momentary illumination" of the prophet and that of the philosopher. Let us leave aside the fact that the text in the *Guide,* II, 38 in any case postulates an essential distinction between direct prophetic and merely indirect philosophical knowledge. Further, let us leave aside entirely that even if Guttmann's interpretation were correct, even then a speculative superiority of the prophet over the philosopher would be recognized and therefore one could not speak of the *identity* of the truths of Revelation with the truths of Reason. But Guttmann's interpretation passes over the *essential* distinction between the "momentary illumination" of the prophet and that of the philosopher, which is postulated precisely in the place he cites. For Maimonides says that the deep, dark night is illuminated for the prophet through lightning bolts from on high, but for the philosophers only through the "small light" that shines (*back*) from pure, gleaming bodies. In our interpretation, we follow the Hebrew commentators (Narboni, Shemtob, and Abravanel). Ibn Falaquera, in his commentary on the *Guide,* III, cites a parallel from Alfarabi that confirms the descent of the image in the *Guide's* Introduction from the Platonic image of the cave and at the same time confirms our interpretation. Only the prophets live outside the cave; only they see the sun itself. The philosophers see only the image of the sun; they have, so to speak, only a remembered representation of it. Cf. text, pp. 16f. and 104f. [The reference to 16f. is evidently a typographical error; it should be to 87f. Also, Lawrence Victor Berman has argued in *Ibn Bājjah and Maimonides: A Chapter in the History of Political Philosophy,* Ph.D. diss. The Hebrew University, 1959, p. 5, n. 4, that Strauss's citation of al-Fārābī as the source of the parallel version of the image is incorrect. He cites a copyist's error as the cause of the erroneous citation, which should be, he claims, to Ibn Bājjah. Cf. below, p. 133, n. 78. I am grateful to Professor Ralph Lerner for bringing this to my attention.]

Notes

72. Guttmann, *Religion und Wissenschaft*, p. 15, and Guttmann, *Philosophies of Judaism*, pp. 200ff. [The passage has been greatly revised from the German edition in the English translation.]

73. Maimonides, *Guide*, II, 25, pp. 327ff.; II, 32, pp. 360ff.; and III, 20, pp. 400ff.

74. Cf. *Guide*, I, 34, pp. 72ff. Since the communication of teachings necessary for life as such is the purpose of Revelation, Revelation thus also proclaims such teachings that are not actually true but are nonetheless necessary so that human life, i.e., living together, becomes possible. Cf. *Guide*, III, 28, pp. 512ff., and I, 54, pp. 123ff. as well as my text, *Spinoza's Critique of Religion*, p. 171, fn. 220, p. 295.

75. Cf. Maimonides, *Guide*, I, 40, pp. 90f.

76. See above, Chapter 1, note 12.

77. Toward the end of *Sefer ha-Emunah ha-Ramah* [Frankfurt a.M.: 1852]; in Guttmann, *Philosophies of Judaism*, see p. 151.

78. Guttmann, *Philosophies of Judaism*, p. 224.

79. See text, p. 78.

80. Guttmann, *Religion und Wissenschaft*, p. 46.

81. Compare to this and the following, text pp. 97ff. The hitherto unpublished investigations of Paul Kraus, which concern the history of Islamic religion and the philosophy of the ninth and tenth centuries especially, bring important further confirmations to the conception sketched in what follows. [The subsequently published works Strauss here refers to include: "Raziana," *Orientalia*, N. S., v. IV (1935), 300–334, v. V (1936) 35–36, 358–378; and "Beiträge zur islamischen Ketzergeschichte," *Rivista degli Studi Orientali*, v. XIV (1934), pp. 93–129, 335–379; and perhaps "Les Controverses de Fakhr Al-Din Razi," *Bulletin de l'Institut d'Égypte*, v. XIX (1936–1937); and "Plotin chez les Arabes," *Bulletin de l'Institut d'Égypte*," v. XXIII (1941), 263–295.]

82. Guttmann, *Philosophies of Judaism*, p. 248 and fn. 11 of II, 4, p. 430. Also compare Guttmann's latest publication, "Zur Kritik der Offenbarungsreligion in der islamischen und jüdischen Philosophie," *Monatsschrift für Geschichte und Wissenschaft des Judentums*, v. 78 (1934), pp. 456–464. [Reprinted in *Guttmann*.]

83. We do not deny, as scarely needs to be remarked, that the problem of "faith and knowledge" is the central problem of medieval rationalism. We only quarrel with Guttmann about the meaning that "faith" has here; it appears to us more exact to say "law and philosophy" instead of "faith and knowledge," since the "truths of faith," which, as Guttmann says, are identical to the philosophical truths

for the rationalists, are, *as* "truths of faith" a part of a more comprehensive whole, namely the Law.

84. Guttmann, *Religion und Wissenschaft;* cf. p. 65 and p. 7.

85. Guttmann, *Philosophies of Judaism*, p. 70. [Silverman, following Guttmann's *"des ungeschriebenen Gesetzes,"* has "the unwritten law"; Strauss cites *"die ungeschriebenen Gesetze."*]

86. Guttmann, *Philosophies of Judaism*, p. 70 ["mere legal technicalities and are not distinguished from the ethical commandments themselves." Cf. above, Chapter 1, note 67].

87. Guttmann, *Philosophies of Judaism*, p. 70.

88. This is confirmed by the way in which Averroism was received in the Christian world. One may characterize Christian Averroism with some right as the herald of the modern conception of the state (cf. G. deLagarde, *Recherches sur l'esprit politique de la Reforme* [Douai: 1926], pp. 52ff. and pp. 81ff.). However, the conception of the state of original Averroism is thoroughly ancient. I would not like to fail to draw attention to the curious conjunction of Plato and Mohammed in Nietzsche's *The Will to Power*, aphorism 972.

89. [Here and in the next paragraph the word used is *"ursprünglich"* and must be understood in the sense of "primordial," not "novel."]

90. Cf. the beginning of Plato's *Laws*.

91. Cf. Levi ben Gerson, *Milḥamot ha-shem*, p. 97.

92. Plato, *Statesman*, 274d.

93. Plato, *Republic*, 499b, and *Laws*, 710c–d.

94. Guttmann, *Philosophies of Judaism*, p. 215.

95. Just with this Mendelssohn shows himself to be a student of *Hobbes*. On Mendelssohn's Hobbism, cf. Hamann's "Golgotha und Scheblimini," *Sämtliche Werke*, ed. Josef Nadler, (Vienna: Thomas Morus Presse, Herder Verlag, 1951), pp. 291–320.

96. Cf. text, p. 108.

Chapter 2

1. [Here as elsewhere, Strauss uses *"aufklären"* for "clarify"; it always carries with it the nuance of *Aufklärung*, i.e., Enlightenment.]

2. Mendelssohn's Preface to his commentary to Maimonides' *Millot ha-higgayon, Gesammelte Schriften*, II, eds. I. Elbogen, T. Guttmann, and E. Mitwach (Berlin: Akademie Verlag, 1929), p. 205.

3. [Strauss uses the German translation by M.J. Müller, *Philosophie und Theologie von Averroes. Aus dem Arabischen übersetzt* (Munich: 1875), with page and line numbers keyed to Müller's edi-

tion, *Philosophie und Theologie von Averroes* (Munich: 1859). The citations here are to the translation of the *Facl-ul-maqāl* by George Hourani in *Averroes: On the Harmony of Religion and Philosophy* (London: Luzac 1961). Hourani's edition also carries the page numbers of the Müller edition for the *Facl-ul-maqāl* here called "The Decisive Treatise, Determining the Nature of the Connection Between Religion and Philosophy."]

4. Hourani, *Averroes*, 1, 7, p. 45.

5. Hourani, *Averroes*, 1, 8, p. 45.

6. Cf. Leon Gauthier, *La théorie d'Ibn Rochd (Averroès) sur les rapports de la religion et de la philosophie* (Paris: 1909), pp. 34ff. Let me refer here once and for all to Gauthier's masterful analysis of the *Facl-ul-maqāl*.

7. Hourani, *Averroes*, 1, 10, p. 45.

8. Hourani, *Averroes*, 1, 14—2, 9, pp. 45–46.

9. Hourani, *Averroes*, 2, 23—3, 2, p. 46.

10. Hourani, *Averroes*, 3, 12—4, 5, pp. 46–47.

11. Hourani, *Averroes*, 4, 11—5, 12, pp. 47–48.

12. Hourani, *Averroes*, 1, 9–13, p. 44; 4, 8–9, p. 47; 5, 12–18, p. 48; 6, 15–16, p. 49; 18, 19–21, p. 62; 23, 7ff., p. 67.

13. Hourani, *Averroes*, 7, 6–9, p. 50.

14. Hourani, *Averroes*, 7, 9–18, p. 50.

15. Hourani, *Averroes*, 16, 3–4, p. 59; 7, 11–18, p. 61; 20, 14, p. 64; 21, 8–9, p. 65; 23, 1–3, p. 67.

16. Hourani, *Averroes*, 7, 16–18, p. 50.

17. Hourani, *Averroes*, 7, 4–6, p. 49.

18. Hourani, *Averroes*, 8, 4–6, p. 51.

19. Hourani, *Averroes*, 8, 14–9, 17, p. 52.

20. Hourani, *Averroes*, 15, 16–18, p. 59; 20, pp. 64–65.

21. Guttmann makes the same judgment in "Elia del Medigos Verhältnis zu Averroes in seinem Bechinat ha-dat," in *Israel Abrahams Memorial Volume* (Vienna: 1927), pp. 194f.

22. Hourani, *Averroes*, 17, 7–9, p. 61.

23. This follows, for example, from Müller, *Philosophie und Theologie von Averroes*, p. 46, 12–15 and p. 49, 1–2.

24. Hourani, *Averroes*, 13, 17–14, 5, p. 57.

25. Namely, the question of whether the creation of the world is to be understood as eternal or temporal.

26. Hourani, *Averroes*, 14, 12–17, p. 58.

27. Cf. Müller, *Philosophie und Theologie von Averroes*, p. 46, 13–17.

28. These passages are collected in August Ferdinand Michael von Mehren, *Etudes sur la philosophie d'Averrhoes...* (Le Muséon, v. VII [1889], pp. 614–623, and v. VIII [1890], p. 13); and in Gauthier, *La théorie d'Ibn Rochd (Averroës)*, pp. 126–130.

29. Cf. text, pp. 70f.

30. Cf. to the following also *Yesodei ha-Torah*, II ff.

31. Maimonides, *Guide*, I, 34, pp. 74f.; I, 50, pp. 111f.; III, 28, pp. 512f.; and III, 51, pp. 619ff.

32. Maimonides, *Guide*, II, 40, pp. 351ff.; III, 25–27, pp. 502–512; III, 52, pp. 619ff.; III, 54, pp. 635ff.

33. Maimonides, *Guide*, I, 28, p. 60, and II, 25, p. 327. "*Maamar Tehiyat ha-Metim*": נצטרך לפרש הדבר שפשוטו נמנע (*Kobez*, II, 10b.). ["We are obliged to interpret anything whose literal meaning is impossible."]

34. Maimonides, *Guide*, I, 35, pp. 80f.

35. Maimonides, *Guide*, I, Introduction, pp. 6f.; I, 33, pp. 70ff.; I, 34, pp. 72ff.; I, 50, p. 112; III, Introduction, p. 415; III, 7, p. 430.

36. The agreement extends significantly farther. It exists above all in respect to the philosophical grounding of the Law. Here, recall only two specific points of agreement that belong to the legal grounding of philosophy. Maimonides teaches (*Guide*, I, 35, p. 81) that one should say to him who cannot understand the interpretation of the text יפהם תאוילה אהל אלעלם הדא אלנץ ("the interpretation of this text is understood by the men of knowledge"). In the same connection, Averroes bases himself on the word of the Koran وما يعلم تاويله الا الله واهل البرهان ("only God and the men of demonstration know its interpretation," Müller, *Philosophie und Theologie von Averroes*, 16, 13). [Hourani, *Averroes*, p. 60, translates "'and no one knows the interpretation thereof except God.'"] Maimonides demands, to be sure, that one inform the layman in question that the passage may in no way be understood literally (it refers to passages whose literal meanings assign corporeality to God). Maimonides explains (*Guide*, I, 33, pp. 70ff., II, 6, pp. 261ff.) that Scripture depicts metaphysical subjects יסדר אלדהן נחו וגודה לא עלי חקיקה מאהיתה: ["... and this in such a manner that the mind is led toward the existence of the objects of these opinions and representations but not toward grasping their essence as it truly is." *Guide*, I, 33, p. 71]. Cf. Averroes to this [Hourani, *Averroes*, 17, 7–9, p. 61]: "The interpretation can only refer to quality, not to existence." For in this assertion of Averroes is implicit that the Law teaches obligatorily only about existence, not about the What or the How.

37. Maimonides, *Guide*, I, 31, pp. 65f.; I, 32, p. 70.

Notes

123

38. Maimonides, *Guide*, II, 24, p. 326. Letter of Maimonides to Rabbi Ḥisdai (*Kobez*, II, 23a).

ואני אומר

שדעת האדם יש לה קץ וכל זמן שהנפש בגוף אינה יכולה
לידע מה מה למעלה מן הטבע...אבל כל מה שבטבע
יכולה היא לדעת ולהסתכל.

39. See text, pp. 44ff.

40. Leon Gauthier, "Scolastique musulmane et scolastique chre-tienne," *Revue d'Histoire de Philosophie*, II [1928] pp. 251ff., and Manser, *Das Verhältnis von Glauben und Wissen bei Averroes* (Pad-erborn: 1911), p. 77.

41. Maimonides, *Guide*, II, 25, p. 328.

42. Hourani, *Averroes*, 13, 17–14, 5, p. 57.

43. Cf. *Milḥamot*, 4, 2–5, with *Guide*, I, Introduction, pp. 5f., and p. 16 and I, 50, p. 111. We cite the *Milḥamot* according to the page and line number of the Leipzig edition of 1866.

44. Levi ben Gerson, *Milḥamot*, 6, 32—7, 4 and 419, 8–15.

45. Levi ben Gerson, *Milḥamot*, 7, 9–11.

46. Cf. text, p. 70.

47. Maimonides, *Guide*, II, 24, p. 327.

48. Levi ben Gerson, *Milḥamot*, 4, 19.

49. Levi ben Gerson, *Milḥamot*, 4, 7.

50. Levi ben Gerson, *Milḥamot*, 4, 11–20.

51. Levi ben Gerson, *Milḥamot*, 4, 14–15.

52. The belief in the possibility of the progress of science is here naturally not belief in the possibility of an *infinite* progress; cf. *Mil-ḥamot*, 356.

53. In this free posture regarding *philosophical* authorities, Levi is in no way distinguished from Maimonides (see *Guide*, II, 22, pp. 319f., II, 24, pp. 326f., and II, 19, p. 308; also from Hourani, *Averroes*, 4, 3–6, p. 47 and 5, 10–12, p. 48.

54. Maimonides, *Guide*, I, 71, p. 80.

55. Maimonides, *Guide*, I, 31, pp. 65f.

56. Levi ben Gerson, *Milḥamot*, 5, 20ff.

57. Maimonides, *Guide*, I, 32, pp. 69–70.

58. Maimonides, *Guide*, I, Introduction, pp. 6–8f.

59. Levi ben Gerson, *Milḥamot*, 8, 6–30.

60. Levi ben Gerson, *Milḥamot*, 5, 33—6, 2.

61. Maimonides, *Guide*, I, Introduction, p. 7.

62. [Here *"erkennen"* is translated as "recognize." Frequently translated "to know," it is closely akin to *"Erkenntniss,"* which is translated throughout as "knowledge" but which carries with it the sense of "cognition/recognition" throughout as well.]

63. Levi ben Gerson, *Commentary on the Pentateuch*, p. 7a. [Strauss may be referring here to the Venice edition of 1547, reprinted in Jerusalem in 1967–68, or to a pre-1480 Mantua edition.]

64. Levi ben Gerson, *Milḥamot*, 7, 12–17 and 419, 19–22.

65. Levi ben Gerson, *Milḥamot*, 441, 24ff.

66. Levi ben Gerson, *Supercommentary on the Topics* Munich Cod. Hebr. 26, p. 326a.

67. [The Active Intellect. This was a conception of the Hellenistic Aristotelians based on the *De Anima*, a separate intelligence that serves to actualize a human intellect, which is conceived of as potential intellect. The Active Intellect is often connected with the sphere of man. My thanks for this definition to Professor Hillel Fradkin.]

68. Levi ben Gerson, *Milḥamot*, 85, 9–26.

69. Levi ben Gerson, *Milḥamot*, 95, 24–30; 190, 2–4.

70. Maimonides, *Guide*, I, 31, pp. 65f.

71. Levi ben Gerson, *Milḥamot*, 189, 1–4; cf. 5, 27–32.

72. Levi ben Gerson, *Milḥamot*, 189, 1–14.

73. Levi ben Gerson, Preface to the *Commentary on the Pentateuch*.

74. Levi ben Gerson, *Milhamot*, 7, 12–17 and 419.

Chapter 3

1. The present essay, written in the summer of 1931, was supposed to be published in its original form—from which the present version does not differ in any important point—in the *Korrespondenzblatt der Akademie für die Wissenschaft des Judentums* (Berlin, 1931) and was accepted for publication by the editorial staff of that organ, which then could no longer publish. It appears in its original form in the journal *Le Monde Oriental*, v. XXVIII (1934). [This version has been reprinted in *Maimonides: Selected Essays*, ed. Steven Katz, (New York: Arno Press, 1980).] The article merely intends to clear up the presuppositions of Maimonides' prophetology. A complete depiction of his teaching or the illumination of all its obscurities is not intended. Most recently [i.e., most recently before this essay was written in 1931], Z. Diesendruck has undertaken a complete depiction ("Maimonides' Lehre von der Prophetie," *Jewish Studies in Memory of Israel Abrahams* [New York: 1927], pp. 74–134). This is not the place for a detailed examination of this investigation or of the rest of the literature.

2. The central position of prophetology and its difficulties are elaborately and emphatically discussed by Diesendruck ("Maimonides' Lehre. . .," pp. 74–79).

3. [The enumeration seems to be displaced. That is, the Part I referred to in this paragraph seems to refer to Part II, which follows directly hereafter, and so forth.]

4. The following remarks about the "medieval Enlightenment" orient themselves exclusively to the representative Islamic and Jewish *philosophers*.

5. Cf. *Guide*, I, 35 in the beginning, pp. 79f. Cf. also Levi ben Gerson's polemic against esotericism referred to above on p. 74f.

6. Maimonides, *Guide*, II, 40, pp. 381ff., and III, 27–28, pp. 510–514.

7. Maimonides, *Guide*, II, 32, pp. 361f.

8. Therefore (see text, p. 85ff.) Maimonides can say that emanation is not distinguished between dreams and prophecy specifically but only by degree. *Guide*, II, 36, p. 370.

9. Maimonides, *Guide*, II, 32, pp. 361f., and 36, p. 372.

10. Maimonides, *Guide*, II, 36, pp. 370–371.

11. Maimonides, *Guide*, I, 34 (conclusion), p. 79; II, 47, p. 409; III, 27, pp. 510f.

12. Maimonides, *Guide*, II, 36, p. 369.

13. Maimonides, *Guide*, II, 38, p. 377.

14. Maimonides, *Guide*, II, 23, pp. 321–322.

15. Cf. especially *Guide*, I, 73, pp. 209f.

16. Benedict de Spinoza, *A Theologico-Political Treatise and a Political Treatise* ch. II.

17. Maimonides, *Guide*, II, 36, p. 373 and 45, p. 403.

18. Maimonides, *Guide*, II, 22, pp. 319–320.

19. [The text has *"nur unzugänglich erfüllen können."* "Unzugänglich" means inaccessible and does not make sense here, though it does when used a few lines above. I have translated it here as though it were *"unzulänglich,"* which fits the context. Cf. text, p. 45.]

20. Maimonides, *Guide*, II, 24, pp. 326–327, and III, 8–9, pp. 430–437.

21. The remark about the stage of the prophets other than Moses is admittedly found only in Ibn Tibbon's Hebrew translation (cf. S. Munk, *Le Guide des Égarés*, 3 vols. [Paris: 1856], vol. I, 11, n. 2) but is required by the whole context.

22. Maimonides, *Guide*, I, Introduction, pp. 6–8. In explaining this passage, we follow the Hebrew commentators; cf. for example, Narboni: "The pure stone, that is the proof and, in general, speculation." Cf. also *Guide*, II, 38, p. 37.

23. Maimonides, *Yesodei ha-Torah*, VII, 6.

24. Maimonides, *Guide*, II, 36, pp. 371–372; cf. thereto I, 34, pp. 76–78, and I, 50, p. 111.

25. Maimonides, *Guide*, II, 36, pp. 369–370; II, 37, p. 374.

26. Maimonides says explicitly that the prophet's knowledge of the future (his capacity to see future things before him as bodily present) is a matter of his power of imagination. This perfection of the power of imagination corresponds to that perfection of the intellect by means of which the prophet gains theoretical insights indirectly, without premises and conclusions. This actualization of the power of the imagination by the Active Intellect as well—thus not just the one that makes it possible for him to present theoretical insights in images—is supposed to have as its necessary condition the influence of the Active Intellect on the prophet's intellect. The Active Intellect acts only upon the intellect, and it works on the power of imagination only by means of the intellect (*Guide*, II, 38, p. 377). This assertion stands in manifest contradiction to the earlier assertion that the Active Intellect works solely on the power of imagination in the case of the truthful dream. The contradiction becomes more pointed if one understands Maimonides' further assertion that the truthful dream and prophecy are distinguished only by degree to mean that in the prophet's knowledge of the future as well only the power of imagination is influenced by the Active Intellect. Cf. note 37 below.

27. Maimonides, *Guide*, II, 32, pp. 361–362; II, 36, pp. 369 and 372; and II, 37, p. 374.

28. Friederich Dieterici has edited (Leyden: 1895) and translated (Leyden: 1900) this text. In the following, we cite the Dieterici edition's page and line numbers. [It is referred to in the following as *Der Musterstaat*, following Dieterici.]

29. Alfarabi, *Der Musterstaat*, 48, 305. Compare to this Maimonides, *Guide*, II, 36, pp. 369–370.

30. Alfarabi, *Der Musterstaat*, 47, 17–48, 9; 8–10; 50, 9–13.

31. Alfarabi, *Der Musterstaat*, 50, 21–51, 4; 51, 14–20.

32. Alfarabi, *Der Musterstaat*, 52, 7–23; 51, 10–12. The preference for knowledge while awake over that while dreaming is also decisive for Maimonides' rank order of kinds of prophecy; cf. *Guide*, II, 45, pp. 395ff., with II, 41, pp. 385f.

33. Maimonides defines prophecy in exactly the same way; cf. *Guide*, II, 36, p. 369.

34. Alfarabi, *Der Musterstaat*, 57, 17–58, 1; 58, 18–59, 1.

35. Cf. Alfarabi, *Der Musterstaat*, 59, 6 and 69, 19–70, 3 with 52, 15–16.

36. Alfarabi, *Der Musterstaat*, 59, 2–3. Cf. Maimonides, *Guide*, II, 36, p. 369.

37. In Maimonides' prophetology it remained especially unclear whether and in what sense he asserted a direct influence of the Active Intellect on the power of imagination (see above note 26). We are now trying to show what consideration of the prophetology of Alfarabi produces in answering this question. Like Alfarabi, Maimonides teaches that in the case of prophetic knowledge, the Active Intellect first influences the prophet's intellect and *"afterward"* his power of imagination (*Der Musterstaat*, 58, 22, and *Guide*, II, 36, p. 369.) Like Alfarabi, he ascribes the prophet's knowledge of the future to his power of imagination (*Der Musterstaat*, 59, 1, and *Guide*, II, 38, p. 377). Thus, according to Alfarabi as well as to Maimonides, in prophetic knowledge—it does not matter whether it is imaginative conception of the things of the intellect or knowledge of the future—no direct influence of the Active Intellect on the power of imagination takes place. But how is it as regards non-prophetic knowledge? Directly following his unconditional denial of direct influence of the Active Intellect, Maimonides presents a noteworthy polemic. He disputes that people who lack intellectual perfection can receive theoretical insights in their sleep (*Guide*, II, 38, p. 378). This possibility was acknowledged by Alfarabi. He teaches that in the truthful dream and in lower prophecy, the Active Intellect also communicates things of the intellect to the power of the imagination. Perhaps Maimonides means the denial of the direct influence of the Active Intellect on the power of imagination only with respect to prophecy as such—and not with respect to the truthful dream—*and* looking ahead to his disputation of the possibility that a man whose intellect is not perfect could receive theoretical insights. Perhaps he denies as little as does Alfarabi that the Active Intellect acts directly upon the power of imagination in knowledge of the future through a truthful dream. Indeed, he even asserts, in explicit language, a direct influence in the case of the (future-knowing) truthful dream (*Guide*, II, 37, p. 374). Speaking against this effort to bring Maimonides' contradictory assertions into harmony with each other by considering his relationship to Alfarabi is the following reflection, which also takes this relationship into account. It is striking that in the passage in which he speaks quite generally of the activity of the power of imagination, Maimonides says that it is the strongest when the senses rest (*Guide*, II, 36, p. 370), whereas Alfarabi, whom he otherwise follows throughout (see pp. 92ff.), says in the same context that it is when the senses *and the understanding* rest (*Der Musterstaat*, 47, 21f., and 51, 15–17). Is this

only a laxness of expression in Maimonides, or is it a conscious correction? If it is a conscious correction, he seems to say that the cooperation of the understanding is required even for knowledge of the future in the truthful dream. Then one could understand his utterance that in the truthful dream the Active Intellect influences only the power of imagination and not the intellect as follows: in the truthful dream too, the Active Intellect's influence on the power of imagination takes place only by way of the intellect, but this influence passes by the intellect, so to speak, without a trace, if the intellect is not perfect (cf. *Guide*, II, 37, p. 374).

38. Maimonides, *Guide*, II, 36, p. 369; Alfarabi, *Der Musterstaat*, 52, 11–12 and 59, 2–3.

39. Alfarabi, *Der Musterstaat*, 46, 7–47, 3.

40. Alfarabi, *Der Musterstaat*, 58, 23.

41. Perhaps Ibn Tufayl's polemic against Alfarabi's prophetology (*Ḥayy ibn Yaqdhan*, ed. Gauthier [Algiers: Imprimerie Orientale, 1900], p. 12) also speaks for this interpretation. A counterinstance would be a passage in Alfarabi's *Philosophische Abhandlungen* (Dieterici edition [Leyden: 1895], p. 75) if this passage and the whole context really come from Alfarabi and not, as seems more probable to me, from Avicenna. Compare this with the passage from Alfarabi referred to on p. 105.

42. *De Anima* V, 6 (*Opera Avicennae* [Venice: 1508], f. 26b); (Fazlur Rahman has edited Avicenna's *De Anima* [Oxford: Oxford University Press, 1959]; *Tis'rasā'il* (Constantinople: 1298), 84; Landauer, "Die Psychologie des Ibn Sina," *Zeitschrift der Deutschen Morgenländischen Gesellschaft*, v. XXIX (1875), pp. 410f.

43. *Avicennae Metaphysices Compendium*, ex ar. lat. redd. (Rome: Carame, 1927), 243s. Cf. especially the translator's annotations, p. 244. The Latin translation of the parallels in Avicenna's *Great Metaphysics* (X, i, ed. Venice, 1508, f. 107b) is downright incomprehensible. I have looked at the original of the *Great Metaphysics* in a Berlin ms. (Minutoli, 229, f. 165b–166a). Cf. also the presentation of Avicenna's prophetology in Ghazzali's *Tahāfut* (Bouyges edition, Beirut, 1927), pp. 272–275.

44. Avicenna also says in the "Risāla fi iṯbat al-nubūwā" (*Tis'rasā'il*, 84) that the prophet occupies the highest rank among earthly existences. Cf. Maimonides, *Guide*, II, 36, p. 369.

45. *De Anima* IV, 4 (ed. Venice, 1508, f. 20b) and V, 6 (f. 26b).

46. Diesendruck ("Maimonides' Lehre von der Prophetie," pp. 83ff.) asserts that according to neither Alfarabi nor Avicenna is the power of imagination constitutive for prophecy. He comes to this assertion

with respect to Alfarabi simply because he does not consider *The Virtuous City*. In regard to Avicenna, he bases himself exclusively on Shahrastāni.

47. Marginal mention should be made of two characteristic teachings of Maimonides that, however, do not concern the foundation laid by the Falāsifa. Maimonides emphatically points out that perfection of the intellect, achieved through instruction and study, belongs to the conditions of prophecy (*Guide*, II, 32, pp. 361–362; II, 36, p. 371 and p. 372; II, 38, p. 378; II, 42, p. 390). With this teaching he moves into opposition to Avicenna, who understands the prophet's capacity for direct knowledge to mean that the prophet does not depend on instruction at all (*De Anima*, V, 6; Rasā'il, 44f.). We encounter this conception in an even more pointed formulation in Averroes: "... one knows that the Prophet (namely Mohammed) was illiterate, in an illiterate, common, nomadic people, which never concerned itself with sciences and to which knowledge was never ascribed, which never occupied itself with investigations about the existing things, like the Greeks and other peoples among whom, over long ages, philosophy was completed" (Müller, *Philosophie und Theologie von Averroes*, p. 94). Compare to this Maimonides' completely different judgment about *his* people in *Guide*, I, 71, p. 175 in the beginning. Averroes cites three koranic passages to corroborate his view. This view is in fact the orthodox teaching of Islam; cf. Alī ibn rabban al-Tabarī, *Kitāb al-dīn-wal-daula* (Cairo: 1923), pp. 48–50, and Alī ibn Muhammed al-mawārdī, *A'lām al-nūbuwwa* (Cairo: 1315) (according to Mr. Abdul-Alīm's friendly information). Maimonides' emphatic pointing out of the necessity for instruction for the prophet thus might be understood as a polemic against Islam. He accepts Islam's assertion of the fact that Mohammed had no instruction at all, but finds that it acknowledges that Mohammed's claim to be a prophet is unjustified.

At first glance, it seems to be of fundamental significance that Maimonides excludes Moses' prophecy from his prophetology. He explains that he does not want to speak a word in the *Guide* about Moses' prophecy, not even by allusions. It is fundamentally different from the prophecy of the other prophets; it is incomprehensible to man (*Guide*, II, 35, pp. 367 and 369). He thus awakens the appearance of wishing, in addition to his explicit reservation about the prophetology of the Falāsifa (*Guide*, II, 32, pp. 361f.), to make a further reservation. Is that really so? Despite his cited declaration, he throws some light on how he understands the singularity of Moses' prophecy. Moses heard the word of God without the mediation of the power of imagination (*Guide*, II, 45, p. 403). He determines this singularity even more sharply in saying that Moses prophesied without parables (*Guide*, II, 36, p. 373). This assertion cannot possibly hold without limitation, for Maimonides not only does not doubt but again and again he emphasizes the parabolic character of many speeches of the Torah. Almost any page of the *Guide* can serve as evidence for this. Let me only point out here that in the part of his prophetology in which he thematically discusses the parabolic character of the prophetic speeches, Maimonides cites passages promiscuously from the Torah and from the books of the prophets. At the beginning of the relevant chapter (*Guide*, II, 47, p. 407), it is explicitly stated that the tool of prophecy, the power of imagination, has as its consequence the parabolic character of prophetic speeches. Insofar as Moses speaks in parables no less than the rest of the prophets, he must have the capacity to express his insights in the form of parables, i.e., he must have command over a perfect power of imagination and make use of that power. One recognizes how Maimonides' apparently contradictory assertion is to be understood if one follows a hint that he himself gives. In the passage in which he says that Moses did not prophesy through parables like the rest of the prophets (*Guide*, II, 36, p. 373), he refers to his previous utterances about this subject. He would seem to mean first of all his remarks in the *Yesodei ha-Torah* (VII, 6). There the "non-imaginative" character of Moses' prophecy is determined in the following way: he heard God's word while awake, not in a dream or a vision; he saw the things without riddle and parable; he was not frightened and confused. Thus what is meant is that he was absolutely *not under the spell* of the power of imagination when he was in the condition of prophetic comprehension. He was not confused by the direct contemplation of the upper world, like the rest of the prophets. This does not and cannot mean that he did not *have command*, in the manner of prophets, over his power of imagination. He *had* to have command over it if, again, he wished to lead the many by speeches they could understand. That Maimonides does not distance himself, with his teaching on Moses' prophecy, from the prophetology of the Falāsifa incidentally follows from Narboni's remark in his commentary on Ibn Tufayl's *Ḥayy ibn Yaqẓān* that Maimonides had taken this teaching over from Alfarabi and Ibn Bajja (cf. Moritz Steinschneider, *Al-Farabi* [*Alpharabius*] [Amsterdam: Philo Press, 1966], p. 65, n. 11). Cf. also Ephodi's remark, which is cited by Munk (*Le Guide*, II, p. 288, n. 1).

48. Maimonides, *Guide*, II, 35, p. 368; II, 37, p. 374; II, 46, p. 406; *Yesodei ha-Torah*, VIII, 1.

49. What follows is based on Ibn Khaldūn's account (*Prolégomènes d'Ebn-Khaldoun* [ed. Quatremére, Paris: 1858], I, pp. 168–170).

50. Maimonides, *Guide*, II, 29, p. 345.

51. Alfarabi, *Der Musterstaat*, 50, 18–51, 2.

52. Maimonides, *Guide*, I, Introduction, p. 12.

53. Maimonides, *Guide*, II, 37, p. 374.

54. Alfarabi, *Der Musterstaat*, 58, 23–59, 1.

55. To understand this "and," refer to Aristotle's *Politics*, III, 6 (1278b 19f.).

56. ["*Ursprünglichste*" again, meaning primordial, not novel.]

57. Maimonides, *Guide*, III, 54, p. 635.

58. Maimonides, *Guide*, II, 40, pp. 381ff.; and III, 27, pp. 510ff.

59. Joseph Albo, *Iqq.*, II, 12 (*Sefer ha-Iqqarim*, II: *Book of Principles*, tr. Isaac Husik [Philadelphia: Jewish Publication Society of America, 1946]) asserts with special emphasis (probably polemically against Levi ben Gerson) that the purpose of prophecy is lawgiving and not knowledge of the future. The extensive agreement of this chapter with *Guide*, II, 39, pp. 378ff. is further evidence for the explanation of Maimonides' prophetology developed above.

60. As Avicenna has explained directly before this, practical philosophy consists of three parts: ethics, economics, and politics.

61. The Arabic text is printed in *Tis 'rasā'il* (Constantinople: 1298), pp. 73f. To produce this text, I used in addition to this printed copy, a Gotha ms. (A1158, fol. 159). A Latin translation that seems to have been based on a more elaborate text is found in the collection of Andreas Alpagus (Venice: 1546), 140b–141a, and there is a Hebrew translation that sharply abridges the text in Falaquera's *Reshith Hokma*, ed. David (Berlin: 1902), pp. 58f.

62. *Avicennae Opera* (Venice: 1508), *Metaphys.* X 2 and *Avicennae Metaphysices Compendium* (ed. Carame), pp. 253–255. The Arabic text of the *Great Metaphysics* was available to me in the Berlin ms. Minutoli 229 (fol. 168b–169a), and the Arabic text of the *Compendium* was available in the Roman edition of 1593. Cf. also Avicenna's "Ishārāt wal-ten-bīhāt" (*Le livre des théorèmes et des avertissements*, ed. J. Forget [Leyden: 1892], p. 200).

63. [Strauss here cites as "*Teile der Wissenschaft*" what was cited above as "*Teile der Wissenschaften*," i.e., as "The Parts of the Sciences."]

64. *Tis 'rasā'il*, 2f.

65. [There is a play here on "*Sendung/Gesandte*" very faintly picked up by "mission/messenger."]

66. *Tis 'rasā'il*, 85.

67. *Metaphys.* X 5 (Berlin ms. Minutoli 229, fol. 174b–175a). ["In-terchange" translates *"Wandel,"* which seemed better than "change," "conversation," or "commerce."]

68. *Tis 'rasā'il,* 73f. See text, p. 101.

69. Steinschneider, *Hebraische Übersetzungen,* p. 219.

70. *Metaphys.* X 4 in the beginning (Minutoli, 229, fol. 171b).

71. The accounts of the laws to be proclaimed by the prophet (*Metaphys.* X 2–5) naturally singly follow Islamic law. Whether and how far Avicenna is also influenced here by Plato in individual cases still needs investigation. I point only provisionally to the following parallels. Avicenna: "the first thing that must be legally determined in the city is the matter of marriage which leads to propagation. The Lawgiver must summon to and awaken the desire for marriage, since through it arise the kinds. . . ." *Metaphys.* X 4). Plato: ". . . what would be the first law the lawgiver would lay down? Won't he proceed according to nature, and with his regulations bring order to what is the first cause of childbirth in cities? . . . Isn't intercourse and part-nership between married spouses the original cause of childbirth in all cities? . . . Then it's likely that in every city it's fine, with a view to what is correct, if the marriage laws are the first to be laid down" (*Laws,* 720e–721a). [*The Laws of Plato,* tr. Thomas Pangle (New York: Basic Books, 1980), p. 108.] Avicenna also points to Plato as a guar-antor for the sentence that speaking in parables and riddles is a con-dition for prophecy. "It is laid upon the prophet as a condition that his speech is intimation and his words hints, and, as Plato says in the book of the *Laws,* whoever does not understand the significance of the prophets' intimations does not reach the Kingdom of God. Thus in their writings the most famous philosophers of the Greeks and their prophets made use of parables and images in which they con-cealed their secrets, like Pythagoras, Socrates, and Plato" (*Tis 'rasā'il* 85).

72. Steinschneider, *Alfarabi,* p. 61. Cf. in general Steinschneider's chapter about Alfarabi's ethical and political writings (pp. 60–73).

73. Alfarabi, *Der Musterstaat,* 57, 13–59, 13.

74. Alfarabi, *Der Musterstaat,* 58, 23–59, 1.

75. Alfarabi, *Der Musterstaat,* 59, 10–60, 11.

76. From here it becomes understandable why Maimonides em-phasizes daring as a condition of prophecy in the *Guide* (II, 38, pp. 376ff.). The talmudic maxim that prophecy only rests on one who is wise, *strong* (brave), and rich does not come into question as a source for this assertion. This also follows from the fact that Maimonides takes this maxim as the basis in a wholly different explication of his

prophetology: cf. *Guide*, II, 32, p. 360ff., and Munk, *Le Guide*, II, 32, p. 263, n. 20.

77. Plato, *Republic*, 485a–487a; cf. also *Republic*, 374e–376c, and *Laws*, 709e–710c.

78. Shemtob Falaquera, *Moreh ha-moreh* (Pressburg: 1837), p. 132. The reference on page 9 of this edition is marred by a typographical error ("31" instead of "51"). [Reprinted as *Shelosha Qadmonei Mefarshei ha-Moreh*, Jerusalem: 1960.]

79. [Strauss uses *"weissagen"* here for "foretell" or "prophesy."]

80. Cf. for example Cicero, *De Divinatione*, I, 41, 89. Karl Reinhardt has interpreted this teaching comprehensively and has tried to trace it back to Poseidonios as its originator (*Poseidonios* [Munich: 1929], pp. 429ff.).

81. [Until now *"Leiter"* and variants have been used for "leader"; this is the only use of *"Führertum."*]

82. Tor Andrae, *Die Person Muhammeds* [Stockholm: 1918], p. 360.

83. Cf. the comments about Philo's teaching on enthusiasm in Hans Lewy, *Sobria ebrietas. Untersuchungen zur Geschichte der antiken Mystik* (Giessen: 1929), pp. 56ff. The Pneuma has the same function in Philo that the Active Intellect has for the Falāsifa and Maimonides.

84. The most important task of his treatise, "Charakteristik der Ethik Maimunis" (first appearing in the compilation *Moses ben Maimon* [Leipzig: 1908], I, pp. 63–134, reprinted in *Jüdischen Schriften*), is to adduce the evidence for this assertion. (In the following notes, we cite the page numbers of the first edition.)

85. Cohen, "Charakteristik," p. 105.

86. Cohen, "Charakteristik"; cf. especially pp. 63f., p. 70, and p. 108.

87. Cohen, "Charakteristik," p. 86. Cohen emphasized the principal clause.

88. Cohen, "Charakteristik," p. 81. Similar utterances are also found on pp. 83f. and p. 91.

89. Therefore, like Maimonides and Averroes especially, they are no less "jurists" than philosophers.

90. Cf. text, pp. 62ff.

91. Cohen, "Charakteristik," p. 87.

INDEX